Getting The Monkey Off Your Back

A COMPREHENSIVE PROCESS OF PERSONAL EMPOWERMENT
BY PULLING DOWN STRONGHOLDS

J. Emil Terry

authorHOUSE®

AuthorHouse™
1663 Liberty Drive
Bloomington, IN 47403
www.authorhouse.com
Phone: 1-800-839-8640

Published by AuthorHouse   05/23/2012

ISBN: 978-1-4685-4160-1 (sc)
ISBN: 978-1-4685-4159-5 (hc)
ISBN: 978-1-4685-4158-8 (e)

Library of Congress Control Number: 2012900502

ACKNOWLEDGMENTS

I thank the head of my life the Lord Jesus Christ for giving me eternal life and guidance through the Holy Spirit to begin and finish this valuable literary work. The Lord has blessed me with tremendous support by placing people in my life that continue to encourage me on a daily basis. Praise God for my parents posthumously Joseph Emil Terry Sr. and Wanda Lee Jackson, step-father Richard Bell, step-mother Naomi Terry, and grand-mother Bessie Jackson for their patience with me through my years of active addiction.

I want to thank my first born child Yosepp Terry for his encouragement, moral and spiritual support throughout the years of our father and son relationship. I thank God for the rest of our children Jaryn Hall, Jaymie Hall, and Janelle Terry for understanding when I needed the entire house to be quiet, because I was studying for tests or writing research papers.

Praise God for Carolyn Williams who was my first Food and Nutrition Professor at Long Beach City College in Long Beach, California. On a daily basis she kept telling me "Joseph you can do it," because each day that I showed up for class I was ready to quit. As a result of her strong encouragement I was able to complete an Associate in Arts degree and ultimately went on to complete a Master of Arts from Southwestern Baptist Theological Seminary in Fort Worth, Texas.

Finally, I want to thank my lovely wife Desiree Terry for supporting me emotionally, morally, and spiritually while I pursued higher education for the first eleven and a half years of our marriage. Desiree also kept pushing me to complete this book and actually conducted the editing on this important piece of work. Praise God!

CONTENTS

FOREWORD

W hat an epic piece of literature produced under the guidance of God, giving clear direction to those whom overcoming has become a life-long and monumental endeavor. The pulling down of strongholds in one's life often becomes an impossible dream, but this book gives help to the helpless, and hope to the hopeless. Whether the setting is the confinement of a Personal Residence, Fast Food joint, Liquor store, Dope-house, Smoke-house, Dope Shooting gallery, Casino, Jail or Prison cell, Wall Street office, the White House, Hollywood or Las Vegas Celebrity dressing room, Worship service, Bible study, or a 12 Step recovery group setting, the reader maybe for the first time after reading this book realizes that deliverance is possible; moreover, that people are not the source but the vehicle by which the source operates and conducts the business of liberation. When people are addicted, obsessed, compulsive, irritable, restless, and discontented they need clear direction, and that is exactly what this book offers. Too many times other's personal opinions and ego is the product that people become adapted to when seeking a solution to their problem(s). Finally when they come across someone who says that there is a solution to their problem(s), then they realize there are conditions to obtaining principles that make the solution work. In the Behavioral Sciences it is the therapeutic process, and that could involve counseling sessions and even medication. In recovery it is the 12 Step recovery programs that offer freedom from addictive behavior. In the Behavioral Sciences there is really no emphasis placed on spiritual principles; but in the 12 Step recovery groups and the literature utilized in the various programs, it is often stated in the program literature that the program is spiritual and not religious in nature. This book is not about religion, but it is about a personal relationship with the One that makes all things possible. Subsequently, the 12 Step groups all utilize the same Steps, Traditions, and Concepts as a plan of recovery and means of operation. Likewise, the Behavioral Sciences utilize various counseling concepts and techniques to treat their clients. In the introductory material of the 12 Step programs it is stated that the program is spiritual, and the name God is used in generic terms multiple times. One thing is for certain and that is, spiritual does not necessarily mean godly. If a problem can be solved by any person of the human race, then one does not need God. On the other hand if one has tried everything she/he can think of and have exhausted every possible source in their attempt to be set free, then this book will lead them to the solution. No matter what the problem may be, sincerely put to the test all of the principles outlined in this book and you shall overcome. This may sound arrogant, narrow minded, egotistical, and self absorbed, but after more than 25 years of active addiction to alcohol, drugs and sex, I have been freed from the obsessive, compulsive use and abuse of these vices for over 24 years. The principles worked for me and many others that I have come into contact with in my pursuit of recovery; and the principles will work for anyone who makes practical application of them in their lives.

J. Emil Terry

INTRODUCTION

In life challenges will loom and individuals often respond in disbelief when this happens, but the Bible warns society of a day that brings about the greatest of challenges. Jesus spoke these words to His disciples, "In the world you will have tribulation; but be of good cheer, I have overcome the world."[1] Are you seeking a solution to overcoming overwhelming challenges, burdens, vices or devices that renders your life powerless and unmanageable? If your answer to this question is no, then give this book to someone who is seeking a solution to all the trouble that plagues their life. Often what plagues mankind is self inflicted, but at some point self awareness must surface and reality warrants personal action.

Here is the hard truth about the solution to all that may plague one's life. Often people go to counselors, psychologist or psychiatrist when they have problems with emotional disorders, alcoholism, drug addiction; and addictive behavior that may include over-eating, gambling, pornography, and other practices not mentioned. These maladies are spiritual in nature and the Bible refers to them as strong-holds.

> For the weapons of our warfare are not carnal but mighty in God for pulling down strongholds, casting down arguments and every high thing that exalts itself against the knowledge of God, bringing every thought into captivity to the obedience of Christ, and being ready to punish all disobedience when your obedience is fulfilled.[2]

---

[1]   John 16:33b
[2]   2 Cor. 10:4-6

The spiritual aspects of life's experiences can be summarized in the fact that everyone is in a spiritual battle. If you are not a part of God's family then spiritually you're dead, and if you're a part of God's family then you're in a spiritual warfare with the devil. If you really want to be helped, please search the contents of this book and do not allow yourself to be offended by what you are reading. Instead of being offended consider this as a strong dose of the right kind of medicine that is hard to swallow but once it gets down inside of you, it works wonders.

Some may seek help through the local 12 Step recovery groups, but many over-look the fact that God is the only one in the business of deliverance. Many of the groups just mentioned pride themselves on being spiritual programs, but there is a difference in spiritual and godly. There are effective 12 Step groups, but those that are effective focuses on the Creator of this universe as their Higher Power. Regardless of what your struggle may be, Getting The Monkey Off Your Back is more than a book for good reading. This literary theological system sets every process of self help, human intervention, and faulty psycho-babble into proper perspective; moreover, it allows the reader to discover a realistic informative source of guidance in being set free.

CHAPTER ONE

The Problem

Identifying the Struggle

"Getting the monkey off your back" is a phrase used in characterizing someone controlled or bound by some type of malady. In most cases the condition exists due to substance dependence; but it may also be a practice that produces negative results. According to Merriam-Webster, the term "Monkey on One's back" dates back to approximately 1859. Merriam-Webster characterized this phrase as "a desperate desire or addiction to drugs—often used in the phrase monkey on One's back; broadly: a persistent or annoying encumbrance or problem."[3] When people are struggling with what the world defines as addictive behavior or an emotional disorder, often the problem is identified as either psychological, physiological or both. When the disorder is associated with substance dependence the malady is recognized as a disease, and this is interpreted by some as rendering the victim helpless and in some portrayals hopeless. Also, it removes responsibility for the actions of the individual plagued by the malady; because when one has a disease she/he is a victim deemed helpless due to that condition. What message does this send to those who make the choice to indulge in and become abusers of alcohol, drugs, gambling, pornography, and other addictive behaviors? Conversely the Bible

---

[3] The Merriam-Webster Concise School and Office Dictionary (1991), s.v. "Monkey."

identifies these maladies as strongholds.[4] There is an old saying that is prevalent in the secular support groups of recovery. Once an alcoholic or drug addict, always an alcoholic or drug addict. What is the nature of the problem? Is it psychological, physiological, or both? Is it spiritual, or all three? Identifying the problem will be the primary focus of this chapter. Discovering the solution will be the objective, resulting in a suggested method of recovery and/or deliverance for the reader.

Nature of the Condition

Destructive behavior is an indication that a person has a heart condition. This condition is not only psychological or physiological, but it is spiritual in nature as well. Listen to the various portrayals of the virulent heart and see if any of these are familiar.

"Do not eat the bread of a miser, nor desire his delicacies; for as he thinks in his heart, so is he. "Eat and drink!" he says to you, but his heart is not with you."[5]

"Yet they did not obey or incline their ear, but followed the counsels and the dictates of their evil hearts, and went backward and not forward."[6]

"The heart is deceitful above all things, and desperately wicked, who can know it?"[7]

"Do not incline my heart to any evil thing, to practice wicked works with men who work iniquity; and do not let me eat of their delicacies."[8] There is sufficient evidence biblically to determine the nature and source of destructive or evil behavior. Jesus said to the Scribes and Pharisees:

"Brood of vipers! How can you, being evil, speak good things? For out of the abundance of the heart the mouth speaks."[9]

---

[4]   Thomas Nelson, Holy Bible: New King James Version, 2 Corinthians 10:4, (Nashville, TN: Broadman & Holman Publishers, 1988), 1020.

[5]   Prov. 23:6-7.

[6]   Jer. 7:24.

[7]   Ibid. 17:9.

[8]   Ps. 141:4.

[9]   Matt. 12:34.

He pointed out to this same group of people that it is, "Not what goes into the mouth defiles a man; but what comes out of the mouth, this defiles a man."[10]

Whether it is what one does in terms of speech or actions it is initiated in the heart and carried out through verbal or physical actions. In fact one must guard their heart against evil influence, since the heart is the gateway to the mind. Listen to the wisdom writer's exhortation:

"Keep your heart with all diligence, for out of it spring the issues of life."[11] There is only one person known to mankind who can replace corrupt hearts, and His name is Jesus Christ.

"Neither is there salvation in any other: for there is none other name under heaven given among men, whereby we must be saved."[12]

When one receives Jesus Christ a tremendous process of transformation is in progress. The immediate transformation changes the spiritual status of the recipient, but there is still the on-going process of progressive sanctification. Progressive sanctification is that process in which the recipient grows spiritually over a period of time. This is based upon his/her life experience as well as time spent studying God's word and applying it to his/her life.

Transformation is Required

The corrupt heart must be replaced, because fixing it will not be sufficient. It must be a new heart that produces positive, pure thoughts and actions. "And do not be conformed to this world, but be transformed by the renewing of your mind, that you may prove what is that good and acceptable and perfect will of God."[13] In this passage Paul tells the reader that he/she must not be conformed to this world, and the Greek word for conformed, **suschematizo** [14] actually means to be conformed to the same pattern, or to fashion one's self according to the world's system or way of doing things. He goes on to point out that one must be transformed by the renewing of their mind. The transformation

---

10 Ibid. 15:11.

11 Prov. 4:23.

12 Acts 4:12.

13 Rom. 12:2.

14 Strong's Greek Dictionary s.v. "conformed" (4964).

that Paul is referring to comes from the Greek word **metamorphoo** or **metamorphiste**, which is the English translation metamorphosis. The word metamorphosis means to change or transfigure; and the renewing refers to a present passive imperative tense, "keep on being transformed."[15] This word transformed or metamorphosis puts one in the mind of an unattractive worm called a caterpillar that turns into a beautiful butterfly. There is a very important factor about this great transformation that takes place with the caterpillar and that is, when it turns into a butterfly it never goes back to being a caterpillar. Once it becomes a beautiful butterfly, it remains a butterfly until it dies, and it dies in the form of a butterfly. The renewing of the mind comes only when the heart is transformed, and when the heart is genuinely transformed the mind will automatically be renewed. There will be an overwhelming desire for renewal.

"And do not be drunk with wine, in which is dissipation [**asotia**[16]—wasteful, riot- like living]; but be filled [**pleroo**[17]—influence or controlled] by the Spirit."[18]

When one is influenced or controlled by the Spirit, that person will have an insatiable desire for renewal. The spiritual condition of the heart can directly impact the spiritual, emotional, and physical health of an individual. If the heart is not spiritually fit, then emotional disorders may be the result. In essence, everyone has a spiritual heart condition upon birth, therefore each person born should at some point in life receive the Lord Jesus Christ so that their spiritual heart condition can be healed. Listen to what the Psalmist says about the spiritual condition of humans at birth and the condition of the heart.

The spiritual condition of the heart at birth:

> Do you indeed speak righteousness, you silent ones? Do you
> judge uprightly, you sons of men? No, in heart you work

---

15   John F. Walvoord and Roy B. Zuck, The Bible Knowledge Commentary: An Exposition of the Scriptures by Dallas Seminary Faculty, New Testament ed., Romans 12:2 (N.p.: Victor Books, 1983), 487.

16   Strong's Greek Dictionary s.v. "asotia" (810).

17   Ibid. s.v. "pleroo" (4137).

18   Eph. 5:18 (NKJV).

wickedness; You weigh out the violence of your hands in the earth. The wicked are estranged from the womb; They go astray as soon as they are born speaking lies. Their poison is like the poison of a serpent; They are like the deaf cobra that stops its ear, Which will not heed the voice of charmers, Charming ever so skillfully.[19]

The condition of the fool's heart:

> The fool has said in his heart, "There is no God." They are corrupt, They have done abominable works, There is none who does good. The Lord looks down from heaven upon the children of men, To see if there are any who understand, who seek God. They have all turned aside. They have together become corrupt; There is none who does good, No, not one[20]

Determining Emotional Disorders

The DSM-IV, the manual used by psychologist and psychiatrist to diagnose Substance Use and Emotional Disorders proposes seven criterions to determine the validity of Substance Dependence. The clinician determines a valid diagnosis of Substance Dependence based upon "a cluster of cognitive, behavioral, and physiological symptoms indicating that the individual continues use of the substance despite significant substance-related problems."[21] Whether an individual struggles with emotional disorders of various types, or are abusers of alcohol, drugs, gambling, over-eating and other addictive behaviors such as practicing homosexuality or involvement with pornography, God associates these spiritual maladies with sin.

Certainly it is not an individual's fault if they are born with an emotional disorder or physical abnormality, but the malady originated

---

[19]   Psalm 58:1-5

[20]   Psalm 14:1-3.

[21]   American Psychiatric Association, Diagnostic AND Statistical Manual OF Mental Disorders, 4th Ed., Substance Related Disorders, Substance Use Disorders, Substance Dependence-Features (Washington, DC: American Psychiatric Association, 1994), 177.

in the Garden of Eden. God told Adam not to eat from the tree in the middle of the garden or he would die. Adam's disobedience in the garden brought about spiritual as well as physical death to all mankind as a result of the malady, which is sin. Not until Adam sinned did anything ever die; moreover, the process of aging did not exist until after Adam sinned. Very seldom do any of the experts identify the problem as being of a spiritual nature unless of course he/she holds the Word of God in high esteem.

Sufficiency of Scripture

There are those who claim to be Christians and yet they don't believe that Scripture is authoritative or sufficient for all things. These individuals do not hold Scripture in high esteem. Listen to what one expert says about the word of God and the significance of Scripture.

> "Beware the person of one book," we are told. For some people the central message of a book becomes a cause; religious books such as the Bible or the Koran are examples. Although causes empower people, we should beware when a person believes that all he or she needs to know is in one book. Such a person remains closed to new ideas and growth. Certainly all taught about helping cannot be found in one book.[22]

This is an example of how confused so called experts are about what the Bible is, verses other books. In response to the statement "such a person remains closed to new ideas and growth," King Solomon told us:

"And there is nothing new under the sun."[23]

Certainly Solomon was better informed than the so-called experts of this post modern era, since the Bible tells us that he was the wisest man to ever live. The Bible is not just a book but a divine living organism within itself. The Bible is God-Breathed.[24]

---

[22] Gerard Egan, THE SKILLED HELPER: A Problem-Management Approach to Helping, 5th Ed., (Pacific Grove, California: Brooks/Cole Publishing Company, 1994), 15.

[23] Eccl. 1:9.

[24] 2 Tim. 3:16 (NIV).

It is for this reason that the Apostle John begins his Gospel with the argument that Jesus is God. He refers to Jesus as the Word.[25] Listen to what the Apostle Paul says about the preeminence of Christ.

"And He is before all things, and in Him all things consist. And He is the head of the body, the church, who is the beginning, the firstborn from the dead, that in all things He may have the preeminence."[26]

Preeminence is defined by Webster as "having highest rank;"[27] and the Greek transliteration of the word *proteuo* meaning to be first in rank or influence,"[28] points out all one need to know in seeking the solution. The reason why people are unable to overcome strongholds is that they refuse to believe in the only source that can deliver them from the destructive behavior that they are ensnared by.

Testing Behavioral Science

Is there a legitimate need for the Behavioral Sciences? There are some advances and methods that have aided clinicians in treating emotional disorders and substance abuse. Some progress has been accomplished through those who practice psychology and psychiatry; moreover, there are medical advances and technology that only a decade ago seemed impossible. Surgeries are being performed without ever cutting the flesh with a scalpel, and there are drugs for everything. If a man has erection difficulties there are drugs that can be taken by mouth to produce an erection. If a man would like to increase the size of his genitals, then there are drugs that will enable him to do so. Women can take drugs to enhance the size of their breast, and there are patches that prevent pregnancy. There is nuclear medicine used to combat cancer and medications that dissolves tumors. However, medicine can be tested and proven to be effective or ineffective. Can the Behavioral Sciences really be tested and proven? Here is the problem with the theory of Behavioral Science. Is Behavioral Science really scientific in nature? Listen to the statements of scholars from the Master's College [Master's Seminary] and their sources.

---

25 Jn. 1:1, 14.

26 Col. 1:17-18.

27 The Merriam-Webster (1991), s.v, "Preeminence."

28 Strong's Greek Dictionary s.v. "preeminence" (4409).

As we noted earlier, psychology is not a uniform body of scientific knowledge like thermodynamics or organic chemistry. When we speak of psychology, we refer to a complex menagerie of ideas and theories, many of which are contradictory. Psychology has not ever proved capable of dealing effectively with the human mind and with mental and emotional processes. Thus it can hardly be regarded as a science. Karl Kraus, a Viennese journalist, made this perceptive comment:[29] "Despite its deceptive terminology, psychoanalysis is not a science but a religion—the faith of a generation incapable of any other."[30]

Conflicts of Psychology

Can Christians trust psychology? According to Bulkley, this question is essential when considering the integration "of psychological concepts and Scripture in Christian counseling."[31] Bulkley goes on to point out William Kirwan's presentation on the issue of integrating psychology and theology in his book entitled *Biblical Concepts for Christian Counseling*. His belief is that psychology is "the science of mental processes and behavior."[32] Bulkley goes on to say "if psychology is a science along the lines of medicine, one could expect a fair amount of agreement within the trade."[33] This is the problem that was pointed out earlier in this chapter concerning the legitimacy of the so-called disciplines of the psychoanalytic model. Bulkley and the sources he incorporates in his book may be the sobering reality that will create clarity in settling the argument concerning the validity of the Behavioral Sciences. One must take into consideration whether or not psychology

---

[29] John MacArthur and others, INTRODUCTION TO BIBLICAL COUNSELING: A BASIC GUIDE TO THE PRINCIPLES AND PRACTICE OF COUNSELING (Dallas-London-Vancouver-Melbourne: WORD PUBLISHING, 1994), 12.

[30] Ibid. 1994, 12, quoted in Bobgan, PsychoHeresy, 23.

[31] Ed Bulkley, Why Christians Can't Trust Psychology (Eugene, Oregon, 1993),131.

[32] Ibid. 1993, 131, quoted in Concepts for Christian Counseling Kirwan, 131.

[33] Ibid. 1993, 131.

is trustworthy, and to give credence to this issue Bulkley has produced a convincing argument.

> Indeed, newcomers normally view psychology, psychiatry, and other forms of counseling as a rather unified discipline. Those who have studied the field, however, know that there are literally hundreds of distinct and contradictory therapeutic approaches to counseling—with thousands of conflicting techniques—all claiming to cure the human psyche.[34]

Unlike the conflicts or contradictions of psychology, scripture is in complete harmony. Scripture has been tested time and time again and it has always proven to be consistent and in agreement regardless of what the issues may be. Historically the Bible is the most accurate document on this earth. The Old Testament is prophecy and the New Testament is prophecy fulfilled. That means what has been foretold in the Old Testament has come true in the New Testament. This is the reason why the Bible is authentic, authoritative, inerrant, infallible, and sufficient for every situation. Is it possible to make the same statement for the DSM-IV and the disciplines of psychology? It appears that the scholars' statements given previously would refute the legitimacy of the DSM-IV, and the disciplines of psychology. This is not to say that every aspect of the theory surrounding the disciplines of psychology and psychiatry are totally wrong, but if the theory cannot be tested no one can genuinely know if it is legitimately working. Therefore psychiatrist and psychologist may present a theoretical process in treating those with inappropriate or uncontrollable behaviors and emotional disorders; but unless the theory can be tested and proven it is nothing more than a presupposition. However, the believing psychiatrists and psychologists are most effective in their practices, because they recognize scripture as being authoritative and sufficient. Scripture has proven to be the ultimate source of deliverance and healing.

---

[34] Ibid. 1993, 131.

Source of Christian Counseling

Another problem arises with the so-called Christian counselor using the DSM-IV, the manual used to determine psychological disorders mentioned earlier in this chapter. There are those who attempt to integrate scripture with the theories of the psychoanalytic perspective. Although the proceeding quote is from over three decades it renders an accurate assessment currently. "Nearly all recent counseling books for ministries, even conservative ones are written from the Freudian perspective in the same that they rest largely upon the presuppositions of the Freudian ethic of non-responsibility."[35] The first problem is the fact that presuppositions are only opinions that in most cases cannot be proven. Finally, failure of one to take responsibility for his/her actions contradicts Scripture. The reason that the Bible requires the sinner and the saint to confess and repent alone requires that one take responsibility for his/her short-comings.

"If we confess our sins; He is faithful and just to forgive us our sins and to cleanse us from all unrighteousness. "If we say that we have not sinned, we make Him a liar and His word is not in us"[36] The Bible, i.e. God's word is the source of Christian counseling. If the source is not scriptural, then how can it be Christian counseling?

Is Help a Reality

The psychiatrist can prescribe medication that helps those suffering with psychotic disorders such as schizophrenia, bipolar disorder, depressive disorders, delusional disorders, attention deficit disorder or attention deficit/hyperactivity disorder and other disorders not mentioned here. Unfortunately no psychiatrist or psychologist has been able successfully to make the claim that those drugs prescribed for such emotional disorders can cure anyone. If medical and psychological advances are being made to help individuals with these problems, then what is preventing the clinician from effectively treating the alcoholic, drug abuser, homosexual, and the criminal committing heinous

---

[35]   Ibid. 1994, 7, quoted in Adams, Competent to Counsel, 17-18.
[36]   1 Jn. 1:9-10.

crimes against society? Why can't these individuals be helped? The first consideration must be whether or not they want to be helped. It is certainly ludicrous to think that people suffering with emotional disorders do not want help. However there are those who participate in addictive behaviors that really don't want to be helped; and perhaps it's due to their insatiable desire to continue in the behavior.

"It is certainly naïve to assume that everyone with a problem wants to be helped. It is also naïve, it would seem, to assume that everyone can be helped."[37] Certainly God can help the helpless and the hopeless. When considering the 42 stories of those helpless individuals in the Alcoholics Anonymous book, it is obvious that only God could help them. When everyone else including themselves had given up hope for their surviving such a demoralizing condition, God intervened.

> For when we were still without strength, in due time Christ died for the ungodly. For scarcely for a righteous man will one die; yet perhaps for a good man someone would even dare to die. But God demonstrates His own love toward us, in that while we were still sinners, Christ died for us.[38]

It is then possible for one not to even seek out God, but that God has already made provisions to birth desire into the heart of an individual to whom He has and is calling. God allows circumstances in the lives of people to get their attention. One can ignore God if he/she so chooses to do so, but the consequences are devastating. God does not want to destroy anyone. Instead He uses circumstances to mold, shape, and build godly character in the lives of the benefactors. Here is a prime example of what God does in the lives of those whom He has called for a specific purpose.

> Now as Jesus passed by, He saw a man who was blind from birth. And His disciples asked Him, saying, "Rabbi, who sinned, this man or his parents, that he was born blind? Jesus answering, "Neither this man nor his parents sinned, but that the works of God should be revealed in him . . ."[39]

---

[37] Gerard Egan 1994, 17.
[38] Rom. 5:6-8.
[39] Jn. 9:1-3 (NKJV).

God's Purpose

Remember that God never allows circumstances nor does He do anything without a purpose. The purpose for this man being born blind was not that God was punishing him or his parents for sinning although "all have sinned and fall short of the glory of God."[40] The purpose in the man being born blind was that God set up a scenario giving Jesus Christ the opportunity to demonstrate His power. By healing and restoring the man's sight, this was evidence that Jesus performed a divine act of healing that could only be carried out by God. Everyone in this man's community knew it was a supernatural act that only God Himself could have performed, and there was no question that the man was born blind. What are you struggling with? Is it alcohol, drugs, gambling, pornography, lying, stealing, homosexuality, adultery, fornication, over- eating, a failed marriage, wayward children, emotional disorders, physical illness, or are you lost and on your way to Hell? If you don't know the Lord Jesus Christ as your personal savior, the Bible says there is the lake of fire and brimstone awaiting those whose names are not found written in the Book of Life?

"And anyone not found written in the Book of Life was cast into the lake of fire."[41]

Getting the monkey off your back perhaps may just be another scenario that God has set up to give Jesus Christ the opportunity before your lost (unsaved) family members, co-workers, classmates, neighbors and yes even your enemies to witness the miraculous saving power of Jesus Christ in your life.

Desire is a Prerequisite

While Gerard Egan appears to give the answer to the question as to whether certain individuals desire to get better or not, there is still this issue surrounding desire. One thing is certainly evident with individuals who continue to do the same things and expect different results, people do not do what they need to; but they do what they want. If this is in fact the truth, then a person's desire will determine their actions.

---

[40]   Rom. 3:23.
[41]   Rev. 20:15.

Can everyone be helped? Gerard Egan appears to believe that there are those who cannot be helped. Is the individual's desire for change deep enough? If so, then destructive behavior can be transformed and everyone who desires can be helped. How does an individual transform his/her desires into that which is pleasing and acceptable to themselves, to the society around them, and to God? First, one must come to terms with the reality that a problem exists. Second, no one is really able by themselves to transform their desires. God can do it for all who will acknowledge Him, and ask Him to work a radical transformation in their lives. If there is no problem then there is no need for a solution. Therefore, the individual continues in the destructive behavior rather than desiring and pursuing the solution to their problem(s). Third, once the recognition of the problem(s) have been established, then the acknowledgement must follow. It's not enough to admit the problem exist and then take no action to solve it. Fourth, the individual must be willing to take personal responsibility for their actions and not blame others or circumstances for their destructive behavior. Finally, total surrender to God is absolutely necessary if God is going to transform the individual's desires.

"Delight yourself also in the Lord, And He shall give you the desires of your heart."[42]

Root of the Problem

Dr. John Babbler, a professor at Southwestern Baptist Theological Seminary in Fort Worth, Texas, during the spring of 1999 made this statement in a class entitled "Counseling with Scripture." "Whenever someone with depression comes to me for counseling, I know if I dig deep enough that I will find sin at the root of the problem."[43] Where did he get such narrow minded thinking? He got this narrow minded thinking from the Bible.

"Anxiety in the heart of man causes depression, but a good word makes it glad."[44]

---

[42] Ps. 37:4.

[43] John Babler, Depression, 1999.

[44] Prov. 12:25.

Living independently of God causes anxiety, because independence leads to disobedience. As miserable as it may be for those stuck in destructive behaviors, it appears that certain comfortable adaptation develops over time and it becomes a way of life for the individual. Eventually these people will do the very things they swore they would never do in life. What is the nature of behavior that drives mankind to participate in destructive activities? Such activities as murder, robbery, lying, stealing, sexual immorality of all types, alcohol and drug abuse and other destructive behaviors are all symptoms of the problem, which is sin. When one deals with the sin issue in his/her life, the symptoms will go away. One must stop focusing on the problem and start seeking the solution. If one really wants to get the monkey off their back, then put the word of God to the test and implement it into one's circumstances of life. Then watch every word prove the sufficiency of scripture in one's life and struggles, and be victorious as an over-comer of life's challenges and plights. To do what was suggested in the previous sentences concerning getting the monkey off one's back, one must stop living a victimized life of their own limited power and start living a victorious life in the unlimited power of the Lord Jesus Christ. Before one begin asking God to deliver him/her, one should establish a personal relationship with Him through the Lord Jesus Christ. Listen, when a person has tried everything and nothing else has worked, why not try God who has all power, all knowledge, and is everywhere at the same time.

Who else could be better prepared to help anyone, except God? If there is someone or something else that can deliver a person out of their trouble, then why haven't they called on this source and why don't they call on them now? They will find that there will be no response to their beckoning call. Only God through the Lord Jesus Christ can genuinely deliver them out of all their trouble. Why don't these people try Him today?

CHAPTER 2

Seeking The Solution

Dealing with Sin

How does one deal with the sin issue in their life? The answer to the question is fairly simple, but people complicate simplistic matters. When one purchases a vehicle and there is a problem with that particular make and model, the owner may take it to another provider of services for repairs rather than taking it to the maker or dealer. If the owner expects to get the best service or solution to the problem, the maker of the product is generally the best source to seek for the solution. Even when people take their automobiles to another source other than the original maker they must use the manual that the maker has produced and made available, so that certain specifications are met. Therefore, since God has made mankind; He knows better how to solve the ills of mankind than anyone else that may be consulted. The Bible then is the manual that gives specific guidance in solving the problems of mankind. Why then would someone seek help from a source that would direct them to anyone other than the Creator? The maker of a product knows more about that product than anyone else. Therefore, it is necessary to consult the maker if one hopes to acquire the most efficient service. Listen to what Bill W. of Alcoholics Anonymous has to say about the solution.

> Almost none of us liked the self-searching, the leveling of
> our pride, the confession of shortcomings which the process

requires for its successful consummation. But we saw that it really worked in others, and we had come to believe in the hopelessness and futility of life as we had been living it. When, therefore, we were approached by those in whom the problem had been solved, there was nothing left for us but to pick up the simple kit of spiritual tools laid at our feet. We have found much of heaven and we have been rocketed into a fourth dimension of existence of which we had not even dreamed. The great fact is just this, and nothing less: That we have had deep and effective spiritual experiences which have revolutionized our whole attitude toward life, toward our fellows and toward God's universe. The central fact of our lives today is the absolute certainty that our **Creator** has entered into our hearts and lives in a way which is indeed miraculous. He has commenced to accomplish those things for us which we could never do by ourselves.[45]

When Bill W. mentions leveling of pride, perhaps he is referring to what the King James Version translates as "humbleness of mind."[46] When Bill W. refers to confession of shortcomings perhaps he is referring to the confession of sins, and this is certainly true of his fifth step in the process of the twelve step program that is found in the chapter entitled "How It Works."[47] The Bible certainly suggests that people confess their sins to one another and to God as well, just as Bill W. recommends in his fifth step. "Confess your trespasses to one another, and pray for one another, that you may be healed. The effective, fervent prayer of a righteous man avails much."[48]

Divine Revelation

When Bill W. mentions finding heaven he could not be talking about anything less than coming to know Jesus Christ as Lord, Master and Savior. Here is what happened leading to Bill Wilson's conversion

---

[45]   Alcoholics Anonymous, There Is A Solution 1976, 25.

[46]   Col. 3:12 (KJV).

[47]   Ibid. 1976, 59-71.

[48]   Js. 5:16 (NKJV).

experience. Bill Wilson's promising career on Wall Street, his law school graduation, and marriage had been destroyed by alcohol by the time he finally found a solution to his drinking problem. While hospitalized at the Towns Hospital several times between the dates 1933-34, he met Dr. William Silkworth who provided care for the suffering alcoholic. During their first experience as Patient and Physician Dr. Silkworth explained to Bill that he had an illness and that it was not a moral failure and had nothing to do with lack of willpower. Dr. Silkworth explained to Bill that people like him suffering with alcoholism experienced an obsession of the mind as well as a physical allergy, and the only solution to the problem was total abstinence from alcohol. This encouraged Bill to some degree and he abstained from drinking for approximately a month, but soon returned to drinking alcohol. Upon visiting Bill at his apartment in New York, his friend Ebby Thacher informed him that he had found religion, and Bill became despaired. Bill had struggled tremendously with God's existence, but appeared to be encouraged after the meeting with his friend Thacher. His friend had suggested that Bill choose his own conception of God, and after hearing such a novel idea Bill experienced freedom from the isolation and fear he felt when it came to God and the reality of him having a relationship with Him. Bill continued drinking after the meeting with Thacher, but the seed was planted and Thacher returned a few days later with Shep Cornell another member of the Oxford Group, which is where Thacher had been introduced to Christ. This gentleman was a bit more aggressive and attempted to encourage Bill to become a part of the group, and in spite of this effort Bill continued to drink. The following morning after meeting with Shep Cornell Bill showed up at the Calvary Rescue Mission under the influence of alcohol looking for his friend Thacher. After arriving he attended his first meeting of the Oxford Group and responded to the altar call. Bill Wilson along with others who had joined him at the altar gave their lives to Christ.[49] It is documented and often shared in meetings of Alcoholics Anonymous that the program is not a religious program, which is true. The most significant thing often

---

[49]   1934 Bill Wilson sober, History Of Alcoholics Anonymous Information (Article featured on Wikipedia, Used under the Creative Commons Attribution/Share-Alike License 1999 - 2011) [database online] http.// reference.findtarget.com.

overlooked is that it is a program that works based upon acquiring a relationship with a power greater than oneself, which is stated in the A.A. Big Book.[50] This power is found in none other than the person of Jesus Christ; moreover, this is not about religion but about a relationship with the power that created this universe.

The Bible clearly records Jesus' words in the Gospel according to Saint John, "I am the way, the truth, and the life. No one comes to the Father except through Me."[51] The Bible teaches us that God is in heaven. "Let your light so shine before men, that they may see your good works and glorify your Father in heaven."[52] What has been defined as the Lord's Prayer but is really the "model or disciple's prayer" begins with "Our Father in heaven,"[53] Is it possible that Bill W. could through inductive reasoning draw the same conclusions that are authoritative as well as historically derived from the inspired (God breathed) Scriptures? The answer to this question has to be a resounding no! There are absolutely too many Messianic overtones in the writings of the Big Book of Alcoholics Anonymous for one to assume that it is a matter of coincidence. One of the greatest antecedents subsequently referring to the preeminence of Jesus Christ is the usage of the word 'Creator' in Bill W's statement above. Not only does he refer to heaven and the divinely spiritual emphasis of the verbiage related to it, but he also makes an emphatic statement that one must receive the Creator in his/her heart. This is an astounding approach to introducing someone to Christ in an unthreatening manner. In no way is this a suggestion that the Gospel message should be delivered with any reservation of compromise, but is a translation of Bill W's approach to delivering a message of deliverance without the conscious awareness of the recipient to distinguish between religion and recovery. To put it plainly, recovery is not about being religious but it is about being delivered. To be delivered though, there must be a deliverer. Remember the last part of the quotation from Bill W's "There Is A Solution," section listed in the A.A. book. "He has commenced to accomplish those things for us

---

[50] Alcoholics Anonymous, WE AGNOSTICS 1976, 45.

[51] Jn. 14:6.

[52] Matt. 5:16.

[53] Matt. 6:9.

which we could never do by ourselves."[54] Bill W. is referring to Jesus Christ when he uses the personal pronoun 'He,' in the previous quote. Notice as well that Bill W. always capitalized the word Creator because he understood the divine preeminence of Jesus Christ. Most people really don't know that Jesus Christ is the Creator of everything that exists. Listen to this argument for the Son being co-equal with the Father and the fact that He, i.e. the Son, is Creator of everything.

> In the beginning was the Word and the Word was with God, and the Word was God. He was in the beginning with God. All things were made through Him, and without Him nothing was made that was made. And the Word became flesh and dwelt among us, and we beheld His glory, the glory as of the only begotten of the Father, full of grace and truth.[55]

It is clear that the Word is referring to the Lord Jesus Christ. In John 1:1 it clearly states that the Word was in the beginning with God the Father. This does not denote the beginning of God's existence but makes a statement concerning the beginning of creation. The Son of God has always existed just as God the Father has always existed.

Jesus Christ on the other hand only existed when He was born out of Mary. The Son of God took upon Himself flesh. Moody gives the meaning of the term from a theological perspective.

> Incarnation. Meaning "in flesh," the incarnation defines the act wherein the eternal God the Son took to Himself an additional nature, humanity, through the virgin birth. By that act Christ did not cease to be God but remains forever fully God and fully man—two natures in one Person.[56]

God the Father gave the order and God the Son carried it out, because He always does just what the Father tells Him to do? "For I have come down from heaven, not to do My own will, but the will of Him who

---

[54] Alcoholics Anonymous, There Is A Solution 1976, 25.

[55] Jn. 1:1-3, 14.

[56] Paul Enns, THE MOODY HANDBOOK OF THEOLOGY, (Chicago: MOODY PRESS, 1989)637-638.

sent Me."[57] "Jesus said to them, "My food is to do the will of Him who sent Me, and to finish His work."[58] If the phrase God . . . "as we understand him"[59] meant that one could choose whatever he/she wanted as their god, Bill W. would have never talked about a change of heart and the acquisition of transformation. Actually the phrase "as we understand him" was only added as a favor to the man whose story entitled "The Vicious Cycle,"[60] was included in the book.

Divine Intervention

Previously in chapter one of this writing an explanation was given for the process of transformation that included the caterpillar and the butterfly. It is clear that transformation is influenced by divine intervention, and a change of heart is absolutely necessary for the transformation to be consummated. Listen to this statement made by Bill W.

> If your man accepts your offer, it should be pointed out that physical treatment is but a small part of the picture. Though you are providing him with the best possible medical attention, he should understand that he must undergo a change of heart. To get over drinking will require a transformation of thought and attitude. We all had to place recovery above everything, for without recovery we would have lost both home and business.[61]

The entire process of recovery is about an individual being delivered or saved from something or some destructive behavior on a daily basis. Remember from chapter one while the word transformed means to change or transfigure, the word renewing refers to a present passive imperative tense, "keep on being transformed."[62] The heart change that

---

[57]   Jn. 6:38.

[58]   Jn. 4:43.

[59]   Ibid. 1976, 248.

[60]   Ibid. 1976, 238-250.

[61]   Alcoholics Anonymous, Big Book of Alcoholics Anonymous (New York City: Alcoholics Anonymous World Services, Inc, 1976), 143.

[62]   Walvoord and Zuck, New Testament 1983, 487.

Bill W. speaks about really derives out of the auspices of the delivering value of salvation. This word salvation from the Greek word "*soteria*, which can mean rescue or safety (physically or mortally): deliver, health, salvation, save, saving."[63] It makes sense that Bill W. would use the type of language found in his program for recovery. There is a difference between being abstinent and clean. King David was indicted by Nathan concerning his adulterous rendezvous with Bath-sheba. He had gotten this married woman pregnant and then had her husband place on the front line of the hottest battle, where he eventually was killed just the way David planned it. Not only was David guilty of adultery, but he had also become a murderer. David the man after God's own heart[64] was now an adulterer and a murderer. Finally, he was compelled to repent. His prayer of confession and repentance can be found in Psalm 51:1-15. The point here is that David never prayed to God because he desired abstinence. He prayed to God for a clean heart because if one's heart is clean abstinence will be automatic. "Create in me a clean heart, O God, and renew a steadfast spirit within me."[65]

Abstinent or Clean

There should be a clear understanding between being abstinent and being clean. There are so many that get involved with some secular support group expecting their lives to change. The problem with their expectations is that they continue living carnal, riotous lifestyles; and while they have abstained from some form of destructive behavior they are still not clean. David requested that the Lord purge him with hyssop. To purge is to remove or cut away. Hyssop was used as a brush in David's day to wash with, and was used for cleansing lepers.[66] We use it today more for seasoning (marjoram) than anything else. When one is clean it means that the corruption has been eliminated and lustful desires although they never are totally eliminated are very offensive to the individual who has experienced this great transformation.

---

63 Strong's Greek Dictionary s.v. "salvation." (4991).

64 1 Sam. 13:14.

65 Ps. 51:10.

66 Lev. 14:4, 6, 49-52.

Reality of Deliverance

Concerning once an addict/alcoholic always an addict/alcoholic! God delivers Believers when they ask Him to do so, but the Believer can always go back to what God delivered him/her from. There was a man laid at a pool called in the Hebrew Bethesda (House of Mercy), waiting for the moving of the water. It was an old superstition that when the water moved the first individual to get into the water would be made well of whatever disease he/she had. Unfortunately the man had been crippled for some 38 years and never made it into the water first. As a result he was unable to receive healing, but Jesus came to his rescue. Jesus asked the man if he wanted to be made well, and all the man did was give Jesus excuses as to why he could not get well. Perhaps it makes sense to the reader now when considering the statement made by Gerard Egan in the first chapter of this book concerning whether or not everyone can be helped. Nevertheless Jesus told the man to take up his bed and walk, and at that very moment he got up from where he was laying and began carrying his bed upon his back. Later Jesus found him worshipping in the temple and told the man "See, you have been made well. Sin no more, lest a worst thing come upon you"[67]

Condition of Relapse

It is evident that we grow worst in our conditions when going back once we have experienced deliverance regardless to how brief the deliverance may have been. God may deliver us from a certain malady, but just as Jesus cautioned the man in the temple not to sin or something worst would happen to him, we must be cautioned as well. This may well be justification as to why addicts and alcoholics alike identify themselves as addicts and alcoholics although they have seemingly recovered.

> When an unclean spirit goes out of a man, he goes through dry places, seeking rest: and finding none, he says, I will return to my house from which I came. And when he comes, he finds it swept and put in order. Then he goes and takes with him

---

[67] Jn. 5:2-14b.

seven other spirits more wicked than himself, and they enter and dwell there; and the last state of that man is worse than the first.[68]

In the chapter entitled "More About Alcoholism, Bill W. gives this exhortation to the alcoholic:

> We alcoholics are men and women who have lost the ability to control our drinking. We know that no real alcoholic ever recovers control. All of us felt at times that we were regaining control, but such intervals—usually brief—were inevitably followed by still less control, which led in time to pitiful and incomprehensible demoralization. We are convinced to a man that alcoholics of our type are in the grip of a progressive illness. Over any considerable period we get worse, never better.[69]

The statement "We know that no real alcoholic ever recovers control"[70] is such a true statement that perhaps it may be an understatement, because no one ever had control to begin with. Total dependence upon God is the only escape from the demoralizing devastation of psychological, physiological, and spiritual deprivation brought about by sin. Remember until Adam ate from the tree in the middle of the garden,[71] the tree of knowledge of good and evil; sickness, pain, and death did not even exist. Finding the solution to the problem is not really the greatest challenge. However, focusing and applying the source of the solution is really the greatest challenge for everyone, not only addicts and alcoholics.

Messianic Overtones

In the ten chapters following Bill's Story there are continuous references made with divine and Messianic overtones that are clearly scriptural in nature. Even Bill W. understood the divinity of Christ

---

[68] Luke 11:24-26.
[69] Alcoholics Anonymous 1976, 30.
[70] Ibid. 1976, 30.
[71] Gen. 2.16-17.

and His preeminence and sovereignty over the entire creation of this world. Bill W. could not have possibly meant for people to choose anything as their God, but understood that not everyone may have the capacity to understand God in His total Omnipotence, Omniscience, and Omnipresence. For this reason Bill W. and the co-authors of the Big Book allowed the phrase "as we understand him" into the writings. Here is the statement made by the man characterized only by the title of the chapter entitled "The Vicious Cycle."

> I don't think the boys were completely convinced of my personality change, for they fought shy of including my story in the book, so my only contribution to their literary efforts was my firm conviction, being still a theological rebel, that the word God should be qualified with the phrase "as we understand him"—for that was the only way I could accept spirituality.[72]

There are several references in scripture where people who sought Jesus did not have a clear understanding of who He was, what He was, and where He came from.

> When Jesus came into the region of Caesarea Philippi, He asked His disciples, saying, "Who do men say that I, the Son of Man, am?" So they said, "Some say John the Baptist, some Elijah, and others Jeremiah or one of the prophets." He said to them, "But who do you say that I am?" Simon Peter answered and said, "You are the Christ, the Son of the living God."[73]

Considering all of the disciples that were with Jesus up to this point especially the twelve, only Peter answered the question as to who Jesus was and what He represented. The other disciples only told Jesus what other people were saying about His identity. They never made a personal statement about who He was, what He represented, or where He had come from.

---

[72] Ibid. 1976, 248.
[73] Matt. 16:13-16.

Once more: The alcoholic at certain times has no effective mental defense against the first drink. Except in a few rare cases, neither he nor any other human being can provide such a defense. His defense must come from a Higher Power.[74]

One Salvation Source

Some of those entering the program of recovery have been raised in the local church but never really had a personal or intimate relationship with the Lord Jesus Christ, and this is the reason why church has never worked for them and recovery has not been a reality in their lives. They must submit to a Higher Power and there is only one true Higher Power. "The tragedy is that people will not accept this salvation freely offered in Christ and instead attempt to earn their own salvation."[75]

According to Boice, people may be justified in their own eyes, but this type of justification does not count. There is God's moral law and He will judge each person by this law. "They must either be justified by faith in Jesus Christ or be lost."[76] Although people may "lead ethically superior lives"[77] and agree that hedonism (the doctrine [teaching] that pleasure or happiness is the sole or chief good in life) is in fact wrong, they are still living morally in opposition to God and will be judged for doing so on the day appointed for judgment. If anyone has set a moral compass for themselves, what is that morality based upon? Is it based upon the Ten Commandments? If so do you keep each and every commandment each and every day? To fall short in any of the Ten Commandments would mean certain condemnation. Are you strictly observing the Sabbath and keeping it holy in your life and practice? Remember if you fail to do so even one time you are guilty of violating the Ten Commandments. Is your moral compass based upon the Sermon on the Mount? Remember once again one must be consistent in keeping every principle and commandment contained in everything written in the three chapters containing the

---

[74] Alcoholics Anonymous 1976, 43.

[75] James Montgomery Boice, Foundations of the Christian Faith, rev. ed., (Leicester, England: InterVarsity Press, 1986), 420.

[76] Ibid. 1986, 420-21.

[77] Ibid. 1986, 421.

great sermon and that would certainly include the "Golden Rule".[78] Anyone that will be honest with themselves and God if not with other people, would not be able to confidently claim before God that they have been strict observers of any of these moral or ethical compasses mentioned. "Clearly, moral people must disabuse themselves of the thought that they can earn heaven. They must admit that they too need God's righteousness."[79]

Prevenient Grace

God has provided the means by which the lost sinner can be reconciled to Him through no provisions of his own. "Prevenient grace is the "preparing" grace of God that is dispensed to all, enabling a person to respond to the invitation of the gospel."[80] God gives the lost sinner opportunity to confess and repent of his evil ways and make peace with Him. "Therefore, having been justified by faith, we have peace with God through our Lord Jesus Christ."[81] Since God has provided the means of peace making for the lost sinner, then that individual should have no problem letting go of offenses of others.

Resentment should not be a stumbling block for those who are forgiven, unfortunately that isn't true in the world in which the Believer must reside. The tendency can be to handle offenses and personal hurts by the mouths and hands of others in the same manner as those that are a part of this world's system. This is the reason why the next chapter is pivotal in the lives of Believers, especially those struggling with various strongholds. Everyone will struggle with some type of a stronghold in the course of their lifetime. Can the principles contained in this book be applied to any challenge in life? Regardless of what the struggle may be if these principles are applied victory is possible. Therefore, prepare to free yourselves from one of the most significant stumbling blocks that will run interference in successful recovery, and will hinder the pulling down of strongholds.

---

[78] Matt. 5-7:12.
[79] Ibid. 1986, 421.
[80] Enns 1989, 496.
[81] Rom. 5:1.

CHAPTER 3

Dealing With Resentment

Removing Stumbling Blocks

Often people who have been ill for long extended periods of time when there are no apparent answers or specific diagnosis may have been guilty of harboring anger, resentment, and an unforgiving spirit. They have visited with a countless number of physician specialists, and none of the specialist can put a finger on the origin of the problem. Resentment causes back problems, gastrointestinal problems, headaches, chest pain, hypertension, hyperglycemic attacks, and anxiety. The Apostle Paul had some strong exhortation to offer concerning resentment.

> Repay no one evil for evil. Have regard for good things in the sight of all men. If it is possible, as much as depends on you, live peaceably with all men. Beloved, do not avenge yourselves, but rather give place to wrath; for it is written, "Vengeance is Mine, I will repay," says the Lord. Therefore "If your enemy is hungry, feed him; If he is thirsty, give him a drink; For in so doing you will heap coals of fire on his head." Do not be overcome by evil, but overcome evil with good.[82]

---

[82] Rom. 12:17-21.

According to Bill W, "resentment is the "number one" offender. It destroys more alcoholics than anything else. From it stems all forms of spiritual disease, for we have been not only mentally and physically ill, we have been spiritually sick."[83] Some of you may be thinking that this is only true for alcoholics, but you need to know that the principles apply in nearly every addictive behavior whether it is sexual addictions, substance abuse, gambling, over-eating, stealing, lying, pornography, and thrill seeking of various proportions.

Silent Killer

Anger often becomes a type of immediate gratification for those struggling with attitude problems. It often drives people just as alcohol, drugs, gambling, pornography, and other addictive behavior. Anger robs the individual harboring it just as resentment turns to bitterness and the recipient carries by choice the heaviest burden of attempting to live with such a yoke about their neck. The person(s) they may be angry with will in most cases not even realize that they are so angry; moreover, the person in whom they are angry with sleeps like a satisfied infant who has just completed feeding from their mother's breast. On the other hand the person harboring the anger lay awake all through the night seething in anger that is causing psychological, physiological, and spiritual deprivation.

> We cannot subscribe to the belief that this life is a vale of tears, though it once was just that for many of us. But it is clear that we made our own misery. God didn't do it. Avoid then, the deliberate manufacture of misery, but if trouble comes, cheerfully capitalize it as an opportunity to demonstrate His omnipotence.[84]

Sin is the Culprit

It is true often people bring adversity upon themselves by their actions. How then does one define such actions without considering sin as the culprit? Sin then is the very element that leads to every type

---

83   Ibid. 1976, 64.
84   Ibid. 1976, 133.

of evil. Sin is the reason for emotional disorders, anti-social behavior, criminal mentality, addictive behavior leading to detrimental outcomes, and alcoholism, sickness, and death. God does allow people to be tested, but most of the time adversity is self manufactured.

Spiritual Warfare

Recovery can be a reality in the life of those seeking it and this will become a reality through the pulling down of strongholds. This world's system is designed to cause Believers in Christ to stumble and eventually fall. From the home or family environment to the corporate environment, the devil is busy at work 24 hours a day and 7 days a week seeking ways to reek havoc and cause destruction in the lives of Believers. The Believer is in a spiritual warfare that must be fought with spiritual weapons. "For we do not wrestle against flesh and blood, but against principalities, against powers, against the rulers of the darkness of this age, against spiritual hosts of wickedness in the heavenly places."[85] Just for clarity a proper exegesis of the previous scripture quotation would read this way from a paraphrased perspective. Our warfare is not with people but with the devil and his demons, who happens to be in churches and in places of employment, in homes, in government, and throughout society. The devil uses people to perpetrate evil upon those whom God has called out of the world into the body of Christ.

> We have been forewarned that an enemy relentlessly threatens us, an enemy who is the very embodiment of rash boldness, of military prowess, of crafty wiles, of untiring zeal and haste, of every conceivable weapon and of skill in the science of warfare. We must, then, bend our every effort to this goal: that we should not let ourselves be overwhelmed by carelessness or faintheartedness, but on the contrary, with courage rekindled stand our ground in combat.[86]

---

[85] Eph. 6:12.
[86] Boice 1986, 171-2.

J. Emil Terry

Clothed and Armed for Warfare

Therefore, the Believer must be fully clothed with the whole armor of God. The Believer must take serious the threat that the devil and his demons pose against those who are on God's side. The devil does not sleep or slumber nor does he take vacations or breaks. While Believers are comfortably resting and sound asleep the devil and his demons are planning a strategic attack and devising evil plans to cause the stumbling that ultimately leads to the detriment of those who opposes his regime.

> Therefore take up the whole armor of God, that you may be able to withstand in the evil day, and having done all, to stand. Stand therefore, having girded your waist with truth, having put on the breastplate of righteousness, and having shod your feet with the preparation of the gospel of peace: above all, taking the shield of faith with which you will be able to quench all the fiery darts of the wicked one. And take the helmet of salvation, and the sword of the Spirit which is the word of God; praying always with all prayer and supplication in the Spirit, being watchful to this end with all perseverance and supplication for all the saints . . ."[87]

J. Vernon McGee points out that Paul previously had used the phrase "I beseech you,"[88] but now he is giving an order to stand firm against the attacks of the devil. In other words, the devil is nobody to play with and he is looking for the opportunity to take Believers out or destroy them. Dr. McGee also pointed out that the girdle was used to hold everything else together, and if a soldier lost their belt they would have a difficult time holding up their pants and fighting the battle. In addition to all of this the Believer's most strategic weapon is God's word and the Believer will be fighting a losing battle without knowledge of God's word and God's word is the truth that holds everything else together.

---

[87] Eph. 6:13-18.
[88] Eph. 4:1.

What is that truth? It is the Word of God. We need people to give out the Word of God and to give it out just as it is written. Today we have many people giving testimonies. We have football players, baseball players, movie stars, television stars, all giving testimonies. Many of them do not know any more Bible than does a goat grazing grass on a hillside. We need people whose loins are girt about with truth. They need to know the Word of God. (I could give you the names of a dozen personalities who have gone off on all sorts of tangents, into cults and "isms.") I admit that some testimonies are thrilling to hear, but they are coming from folks who are standing there about to lose all their spiritual garments! They are not girded about with truth, which is the Word of God.[89]

The list of armor continues with the breastplate of righteousness. Look at what this commentator says about the breastplate.

The breastplate was usually a tough, sleeveless piece of leather or heavy material with animal horn or hoof pieces sewn on, covering the soldier's full torso, protecting his heart and other vital organs. Because righteousness, or holiness, is such a distinctive characteristic of God Himself, it is not hard to understand why that is the Christian's chief protection against Satan and communion with Jesus Christ, His own righteousness produces in them the practical, daily righteousness that becomes their spiritual breastplate. Lack of holiness, on the other hand, leaves them vulnerable to the great enemy of their souls.[90] "And having shod your feet with the preparation of the gospel of peace;"[91]

---

[89] J. Vernon McGee, THRU THE BIBLE, vol. 5, The Soldier's Protection (Nashville: Thomas Nelson Publishers, 1983), Eph. 6:14-15.

[90] John MacArthur, MacArthur Study Bible, (Nashville-London-Vancouver-Melbourne: WORD BIBLES, 1997), Eph. 6;14 study notes

[91] Eph. 6:15.

According to Dr. MacArthur, Roman soldiers wore boots with nails in the soles for traction to grip the ground when in battle.[92] Concerning the next article of the armor that reads "above all, taking the shield of faith with which you will be able to quench all the fiery darts of the wicked one."[93] Dr. MacArthur says this rendering refers to a large shield (2.5 X 4.5 ft.) used to protect the entire body. He goes on to point out that the faith the Apostle Paul refers to is not Christian as suggested in Eph. 4:13, but a basic trust in God. This basic trust is characterized by the phrase "above all," and is necessary to protect the Believer from the temptation created by all types of sin. This temptation causes the Believer to become vulnerable to the desires and lust the devil creates to lead Believers astray ultimately, resulting in sin. Fiery darts are like flaming arrows shot by the enemy, and repelled by the shield. "And take the helmet of salvation, and the sword of the Spirit, which is the word of God."[94] The devil cannot eliminate the reality of the Believer's salvation, so the only other way of attacking the Believer is through doubt and discouragement. So the devil attacks Believers through their thoughts as well as temptation through lust and desires. Also, if the devil can succeed in discouraging the Believer then their witness will be weak and possibly non-existent. If the Believer buys into the doubt, then the devil could possibly cause the Believer to even doubt their salvation. The helmet guards against stinking thinking. The sword of the spirit is the word of God. God's word is armed and loaded and sometimes referred to as a 66 shooter. It can be used as an offensive or defensive weapon in the spiritual warfare that the Believer encounters in their Christian experience. Of course prayer is also a weapon that many Believer's don't use as a first resort. When they have tried everything else and have exhausted all other sources of help and those sources cannot help, then many Believers will resort to prayer. Just think about it, if all that energy, effort, and perseverance was directed toward prayer initially much would be accomplished. "Praying always with all prayer and supplication in the Spirit, being watchful to this end with all perseverance and supplication for all the saints—"[95]

---

[92] MacArthur Study Bible, 1997, Eph. 6:15 study notes.
[93] Eph. 6:16.
[94] Eph. 6:17.
[95] Ibid. 6:18.

Just to emphasize the effectiveness of prayer this passage is a prime example of what prayer can and will accomplish.

> Is anyone among you suffering? Let him pray. Is anyone cheerful? Let him sing psalms. Is anyone among you sick? Let him call for the elders of the church, and let them pray over him, anointing him with oil in the name of the Lord. And the prayer of faith will save the sick, and the Lord will raise him up. And if he has committed sins, he will be forgiven. Confess your trespasses to one another, and pray for one another, that you may be healed. The effective, fervent prayer of a righteous man avails much.[96]

In the previous scripture quotation the indication of effective prayer is predicated upon the prayer of the righteous person. This means that one must be repentant if God will hear and answer that person's prayer, unless of course that individual is praying for salvation. In the case of one praying for salvation, God always hears and answer the prayer to receive Jesus Christ as Savior. "All that the Father gives Me will come to Me, and the one who comes to Me I will by no means cast out."[97] The person that has no personal relationship with God does not have the privilege of prayer outside of praying for salvation. "The Lord is far from the wicked, But He hears the prayer of the righteous."[98]

Repentance is Recovery

Each time the godly person sins recovery happens through confession and repentance. The godly are simply those who have received Jesus Christ as their personal Savior. Through confession as one agrees with God that he/she is a sinner, that Jesus is Lord over all, whether all people want Him to be or not; and that He rose from the dead, and asking Him to be his/her Savior substantiates a genuine relationship with the Godhead. This establishes the one who is the confessor, as a Believer in Christ. Even after this process takes place Believers have

---

[96] James 5:13-16.

[97] Jn. 6:37.

[98] Prov. 15:29.

the propensity to sin. "If we confess our sins, He is faithful and just to forgive us our sins and to cleanse us from all unrighteousness."[99] This is an indication that when people come to Christ and surrender their lives they may still from time to time fall short of God's requirement for godly living.

> My little children, these things I write to you, so that you may not sin. And if anyone sins, we have an Advocate with the Father, Jesus Christ the righteous. And He Himself is the propitiation for our sins, and not for ours only but also for the whole world.[100]

Believer's Defender

The word in the previous quote Advocate in the original language is the word ***parakletos***,[101] which in the English language means intercessor, consoler, and comforter. Some scholars actually translate Advocate as meaning defense attorney. Also, the word propitiation in the original language is the word ***hilasmos***,[102] which means atonement or expiator. This means that Jesus Himself has made those of us who have and will receive Him to be at one with God by satisfying the demands that God has on sin. What are the demands of God on sin? Remember in chapter 2 of this book it was pointed out that in the Garden of Eden God told Adam that he would die if he ate from the tree in the middle of the garden.[103] Also, the prophet Ezekiel prophesied saying that "Behold, all souls are Mine; The soul of the father As well as the soul of the son is Mine; The soul who sins shall die."[104] Simply put, every soul belongs to God the Father and any soul that sins will be put to death. Jesus died in place of everyone since every human being is guilty of sin, and sin carries a death sentence. "For the wages of sin is death, but the gift

---

[99] 1 Jn. 1:9.

[100] 1 Jn. 2:1-2.

[101] Strong's Greek Dictionary s.v. "advocate" (3875).

[102] Ibid. s.v. "propitiation" (2434).

[103] Gen. 2:17.

[104] Ezek. 18:4.

of God is eternal life in Christ Jesus our Lord."[105] God is full of mercy and grace and have made provisions for those who may sin, but it is a dangerous undertaking to practice sin.

> If anyone sees his brother sinning a sin which does not lead to death, he will ask, and He will give him life for those who commit sin not leading to death. There is sin leading to death. I do not say that he should pray about that. All unrighteousness is sin, and there is sin not leading to death."[106]

Sin Makes Recovery Necessary

The previous scripture quote is not addressing intermittent sins but actually addresses the issue of practicing sin. If one commits sin that does not lead to death and does not continue practicing that specific sin, then death will not occur from that particular sin. All sin is wrong but if an individual continues practicing a particular sin that sin may cost that individual his/her life. Recovery is not only for addicts and alcoholics but Christians who simply commit sin, because sin is similar to an addictive behavior. People say that certain activities are fun although they may be sinful. Isn't it tragic to lose your life over a few moments of pleasure, because that is exactly what many people do that is deceived into thinking that they are just having fun when sinning against God. These are the compromising actions of those who live any way they want, then blame God when something terrible happens to them or their loved ones. Listen to the writer of Hebrews addressing the compromise of those deceived by sin: "choosing rather to suffer affliction with the people of God than to enjoy the passing pleasures of sin . . ."[107] The writer of Hebrews is addressing the faith of Moses when he was a part of Pharaoh's household. When Moses became an adult or as some would say reached the age of accountability, he refused to be called the son of Pharaoh. He could have continued living the life of a prince, but instead he rebuked that lifestyle to live for the Lord. Remember what happened to the Egyptian regime when Moses

---

[105] Rom. 6:23.

[106] 1 Jn. 5:16-17.

[107] Heb. 11:25.

returned from Midian. He told Pharaoh to let God's people go and when Pharaoh refused to do so, Moses called out to God and 10 plagues went forth. There was the plague of (1) bloody water, (2) frogs, (3) lice, (4) flies (5) livestock diseased (6) boils, (7) hail, (8) locust, (9) darkness, (10) death of the firstborn.[108] If Moses would have taken advantage of living a life of materialism and enjoying the pleasures of sin, he would not have been the messenger of deliverance for the people of God, but he would have been one of the victims of the 10 plagues.

Detriment of Resentment

When people struggle with resentment for an extended period of time it eventually results in bitterness. Bitterness produces the compromising of moral character, causing individuals to slide into spiritual depravation that ultimately leads them into "exhibiting intense animosity."[109] Also, the individual harboring bitterness experiences an emotional and physical decline usually "accompanied by severe pain and suffering."[110] Someone may be questioning the validity of these statements made concerning bitterness; but consider King Saul's resentment toward David, and how it led to his irrational behavior. David was alright with King Saul when he conquered the uncircumcised Philistine named Goliath. Remember Goliath was a 9 foot, 9 inch giant who wore a coat of armor weighing 125 pounds; moreover, the head of his spear weighed 15 pounds and he was a skilled warrior referred to as a champion.[111] David had been instructed by Jesse his father to take food to three of the oldest of eight brothers who were on the battlefield. As David was approaching he heard the uncircumcised Philistine making threats to the Israelites, and his brothers were among those who were supposed to be defending the honor of their God Jehovah. David was willing to take on the champion after observing the entire Israelite army's dreadful fear of the giant. Not only did Eliab David's oldest brother insult him, but King Saul told David that he was not able to go against the giant. David was just a youth and the giant was a man

---

[108]   Ex. 7-11.

[109]   The Merriam-Webster (1991), s.v. "bitter."

[110]   Ibid. (1991), s.v. "bitter."

[111]   1 Sam. 17:4-7.

of war from his youth up and the giant was a seasoned adult. This story is well known and is really just a reminder to the reader of what transpired when David met the giant face to face. David was armed with a sling shot and 5 smooth stones.[112] Some scholars say that David had 5 stones just in case the giant's four brothers came to his defense. David explained to King Saul how he took a lamb out of the mouth of a lion and a bear when one or the other attacked the sheep fold. "I went out after it and struck it, and delivered the lamb from its mouth; and when it arose against me, I caught it by its beard, and struck and killed it."[113] David took down the giant with one smooth stone and delivered his head to King Saul.[114] After David defeated the giant, King Saul was impressed with him and wanted to know the identity of his father. Jonathan, the son of King Saul developed a love for David like that of a brother. After David defeated the giant, King Saul place him over all the army and the servants, and wherever King Saul told David to go he did and behaved wisely. Upon returning home from the slaughter of the Philistine, women out of all the cities of Israel came "singing and dancing, to meet King Saul, with tambourines, with joy, and with musical instruments. So the women sang as they danced, and said: "Saul has slain his thousands, And David his ten thousands."[115] King Saul became very angry when he heard the singing women praising David for having killed 10,000, and said that they have ascribed to David 10,000 and to me only 1,000. King Saul began experiencing that compromise of moral character. The Bible states that from that day forward King Saul eyed David. This is the day when resentment was born in the heart and mind of King Saul. It didn't take long for bitterness to set in, because it was the very next day that the distressing spirit from God came upon Saul.[116] King Saul was so bitter that he threw a spear at David while he was playing music to sooth the King's heart and mind. The Bible says that King Saul's thoughts were to pin David against the wall, but David escaped twice.

---

[112] Ibid. 17:40.

[113] Ibid. 17:35.

[114] Ibid. 17:23-57.

[115] 1 Sam. 18:6-7.

[116] 1 Sam. 18:8-10.

> For those who live according to the flesh set their minds on the things of the flesh, but those who live according to the Spirit, the things of the Spirit. For to be carnally minded is death, but to be spiritually minded is life and peace. Because the carnal mind is enmity against God; for it is not subject to the law of God, nor indeed can be. So then, those who are in the flesh cannot please God.[117]

Here is where the spiritual depravation develops: King Saul began to fear David because the Lord was with him, but He had departed from King Saul. David had the opportunity to kill King Saul, but spared his life although he did cut off a piece of his rob. David was convicted in his spirit for just cutting off a piece of King Saul's robe.[118] What a man of spiritual influence. David certainly dealt with any anger he may have had where King Saul was concerned. When anger is not dealt with properly it grows into resentment. Resentment festers and develops into bitterness. Bitterness causes emotional, physical, and ultimately spiritual depravation. King Saul was emotionally disturbed. King Saul had to have a physical infirmity or weakness due to the stress of constantly being in fear of David although David had not threatened the King at all. King Saul had 85 priests put to death because they would not give David up to him. Then King Saul killed men, women and children in Nob, the city of priest.[119] Someone reading this chapter is in denial about the detriment of resentment. This person is saying to themselves, 'I haven't killed anyone, and I haven't even attempted to do so.' If one had it their way only God knows what he/she would wish upon the individual(s) who has hurt them. Maybe they damaged his/her reputation, stole his/her spouse, or cheated him/her out of that great employment opportunity or promotion. What is the monkey on your back? Is it anger, resentment, bitterness, alcohol, drugs, gambling, sexual immorality, stealing, lying, over-eating, greed, jealousy, envy, or some deep dark secret(s)? Do you really want to get the monkey off your back? The next chapter will explain why forgiveness is necessary if one hopes to experience the reality of a successful recovery.

---

[117]   Rom. 8:5-8.

[118]   1 Sam. 24:4-5.

[119]   1 Sam. 22:17-19.

CHAPTER 4

Element Of Forgiveness

Prayer, Forgiveness, Fellowship

Forgiveness comes through prayer consisting of confession and repentance, and general prayer is really for Believers. The only prayer that God hears from an Unbeliever is the prayer of confession and repentance to receive Jesus Christ. "The Lord is far from the wicked, But He hears the prayer of the righteous."[120] The word wicked in the previous quotation is a reference to the ungodly or the Unbeliever. The word righteous signifies one being in right standing with God. After an individual receives the Lord Jesus Christ through a prayer of confession and repentance, God hears and answers all the converted individual's prayers thereafter. It has been determined by some scholars that those who are genuine Believers in Christ, when praying God answer all their prayers. God either answers yes, no, or wait.

Types of Prayer

There are prayers offered for various reasons. There are prayers of Thanksgiving (Giving of thanks to God); Supplication (supplying a need); Intercessory (praying for others); Confession and Repentance (establishing right relations with God for Unbelievers or right fellowship with God for those who are already Believers); Deliverance (prayer for

---

[120]   Prov. 15:29.

God to deliver from something or someone). David prayed precatory prayers wishing for God to kill his enemies. Here is an example of one precatory prayer that David requested of God:

> For without cause they have hidden their net for me in a pit, Which they have dug without cause for my life. Let destruction come upon him unexpectedly. And let his net that he has hidden catch himself; Into that very destruction let him fall.[121]

Hopefully no Believer is praying this type of prayer today. Instead prayer offered up for enemies should be with the expectation that if they are not saved, by the grace of God they will come to know the Lord Jesus Christ as their personal Lord, Master, and Savior.

Forgiveness Unleashes Blessings

Extending and receiving forgiveness is essential for the Believer. If anyone is unwilling to forgive then forgiveness is withheld from that individual that is unwilling to forgive. There are those who believe that forgiveness should be of a subjective nature or extended based upon the offense committed. Or if someone commits the same offense too many times or the offense is of a really heinous nature then forgiveness should be withheld. Listen to the words of Jesus recorded by St. Luke as Jesus dealt with the Disciples on the subject of forgiveness:

"Take heed to yourselves, If your brother sins against you, rebuke him; and if he repents, forgive him. And if he sins against you seven times in a day, and seven times in a day returns to you saying, I repent, you shall forgive him."[122]

There are many who know and quote the prayer that Jesus taught the Disciples in the synoptic gospels. This prayer has been referred to as the Lord's Prayer, but in reality it is the Disciple's prayer, and Jesus was teaching them how to pray. Some editors and scholars have identified it as the "Model Prayer,"[123] as stated in an earlier chapter. In this one portion of the prayer Jesus instructs the Disciples to pray in

---

[121] Ps. 35:7-8.

[122] Luke 17:3-4.

[123] Walvoord and Zuck, New Testament 1983, 32.

this manner: "And forgive us our debts, As we forgive our debtors."[124] How is it possible that people can say the words contained in this portion of the prayer and never consider that they are telling God to forgive them only if they are willing to forgive others? It is then logical that no one in their right mind would withhold forgiveness that pray and understand the prayer that Jesus taught the Disciples to pray. In addition to this the blessings that the individual may be praying for God to supply are cut off as well.

> Therefore I say to you, whatever things you ask when you pray believe that you receive them, and you will have them. "And whenever you stand praying, If you have anything against anyone, forgive him, that your Father in heaven may also forgive you your trespasses."[125]

Therefore one should be quick to forgive as to activate the heavenly blessings meant for those who are obedient to God's command. Please do not forget that forgiveness is necessary not only for the good of the one needing to be forgiven, but by the one willing to extend forgiveness. God does hear and answer prayer but often the one praying may hinder the response of God in delivering or providing the request because of broken fellowship. Right fellowship has to be genuine on a horizontal level if it is going to be a reality on a vertical level. This merely means that one must have right fellowship with people if they are going to be in right fellowship with God. Make peace when possible with all those whom broken fellowship exist. Do not harbor anger, resentment, bitterness or an unforgiving spirit. This will destroy right fellowship with the Godhead, and cause your blessings to go unclaimed. Furthermore, the Believer is called to serve and it is impossible for one to serve God unless he/she serves people. God does not need anything anyone has to offer, because He already owns everything. One can only serve God by serving other people and harboring an unforgiving spirit hinders the effectiveness of service to others. When one harbors an unforgiving spirit that individual is self-centered.

---

[124] Matt. 6:12.
[125] Mark 11:24-26.

One can hardly be an effective servant if he/she is self-centered. Only when one is Christ-centered does he/she embrace the moral, ethical, and ultimately the love that forgiveness represents. "If someone says, "I love God," and hates his brother, he is a liar, for he who does not love his brother whom he has seen, how can he love God whom he has not seen?"[126] How then can anyone who does not love his brother or sister be effective in their service to others? God has called every Believer in Christ to service, and service requires love. The type of love John is talking about is agape or in the original language *agapao*,[127] which means to love in a social or moral sense. This type of love denotes a responsibility or an obligation to love without expecting to be loved. Some scholars may define agape as the type of love that characterizes the Godhead and is extended with no strings attached. It is easy to love someone who loves you first or loves you back, but to love with no expectation of being loved is the type of love that John is talking about in this chapter. It is impossible to share this type of love with anyone unless God's spirit of love dwells in the one extending unconditional love. It is the type of love that God has for humanity. "No one has seen God at any time. If we love one another, God abides in us, and His love has been perfected in us. By this we know that we abide in Him, and He in us, because He has given us of His Spirit."[128] Since "God is love . . ."[129] and has "given us of His Spirit,"[130] it is possible for a Believer to love unconditionally. God loves sinners as much as He loves those who have a personal relationship with His Son.

> In this the love of God was manifested toward us, that God has sent His only begotten Son into the world, that we might live through Him. In this is love, not that we loved God, but that He loved us and sent His Son to be the propitiation for our sins.[131]

---

[126]   1 Jn. 4:20.

[127]   Strong's Greek Dictionary s.v. "love" (25).

[128]   1 Jn. 4:12-13.

[129]   Ibid. 4:8b.

[130]   Ibid. 4:13c.

[131]   Ibid. 4:9-10.

It is impossible for anyone to love unconditionally without the Spirit of the living God resting, ruling, and abiding in that person. While God loves sinners equally as much as He loves Believers, only those who believe will have eternal life. "These things I have written to you who believe in the name of the Son of God, that you may know that you have eternal life, and that you may continue to believe in the name of the Son of God."[132] Can one still love when someone has betrayed or hurt him/her? Or does one love people that only treat them right and agree with the way they would like things to be?

Love, Integrity, Credibility

Here is a perfect example of what genuine love characterizes. Joseph was one of Jacob's (Israel) sons and the Bible says that Jacob loved Joseph more than any of his other children, and even made a special coat of many colors. Joseph told his brothers about a dream he had that he would reign over them. It wasn't enough that their father loved him the most and had given him a special coat, now he was boasting about how great he was going to be. Not only was he going to be great but they would bow to him. This angered Joseph's brothers and they conspired to kill him. Reuben convinced the others not to kill Joseph but to merely drop him into a pit. As Joseph's brothers were eating lunch and realized that Joseph was of no profit to them in the pit they sold him to a group of Ishmaelites that was passing through that region and they took Joseph to Egypt. Joseph's brothers took his coat of many colors and killed a baby goat and soaked the coat in the goat's blood to make it appear as if Joseph had been eaten alive by a wild beast. Joseph was a slave in Egypt where Potiphar an officer of Pharaoh bought him from the Ishmaelites. Potiphar could see that the Lord was with Joseph and made all that he did to prosper. Therefore Joseph found favor in his sight and Potiphar made him overseer of his house and all that he owned. From this time the Lord blessed the house of Potiphar because Joseph was present in that house.

All that Potiphar had was under Joseph's control except for the food that Potiphar ate. Now after Potiphar had appointed Joseph steward over all he possessed, his wife attempted to seduce Joseph. Joseph reminded

---

[132]   Ibid. 5:13.

Potiphar's wife that he was appointed steward over everything except her. Joseph was handsome and Potiphar's wife asked him to sleep with her, but when Joseph refused she falsely accused him of attempting to rape her. As a result Joseph was placed in prison by Potiphar. While in prison Joseph met two prisoners that were concerned about their fate due to dreams they had, so Joseph interpreted the dreams. The butler received a favorable report from Joseph, when he told him that Pharaoh was going to lift up his head and restore him. The baker on the other hand was told by Joseph that Pharaoh was going to cut off his head and feed his body to the birds. Two years later Pharaoh had a dream and naturally Joseph was the man with the ability to best interpret the dream. After Joseph interpreted this dream that would prophesy to Pharaoh of the impending famine, Pharaoh promoted Joseph and he became the second man in charge only to Pharaoh himself over all of Egypt. Now even Potiphar would have to answer to Joseph. Pharaoh gave Joseph the name Zaphnath-Asenath,[133] which means as accurately as can be interpreted "the deity lives and speaks."[134] Joseph had now become a lord to be held in high esteem.

Epitome of a Forgiving Spirit

Take note that Joseph never displayed or appeared to harbor anger, resentment or an unforgiving spirit toward his brothers or Potiphar and his wife, although Joseph had been sold into slavery and unjustly imprisoned. When the famine took its toll on the world during Joseph's reign as the Prime minister over all of Egypt. Joseph was responsible for issuing the food to what seemingly was the entire world at that time and was reunited with his brothers in the process. He did not harbor anger, resentment or bitterness neither did he harbor an unforgiving spirit toward them although they had a desire to kill Joseph. Instead Joseph gave them money and food and told them that while what they did was meant for evil God meant it for good. Not only was Joseph a man of forgiveness, grace and mercy, he proved to be a man of integrity and credibility.[135] Joseph was not only concerned about his reputation,

---

[133] Gen. 41:45.

[134] The Eerdmans Bible Dictionary s.v. "Zaphenath-Paneah" (1081).

[135] Gen. 37-47:12.

but he was more concerned about God's opinion of him more than he was concerned about what people thought about his actions. Look at Joseph's response to Potiphar's wife: "There is no one greater in this house than I, nor has he kept back anything from me but you, because you are his wife. How then can I do this great wickedness, and sin against God?"[136] Joseph had a good name and his word was credible. "A good name is to be chosen rather than great riches, Loving favor rather than silver and gold."[137]

The Social Ills of Unforgivingness

Many have been affected by the brutality that racism perpetrates against those that are of a different skin color or ethnic background. Most people consider racism something that only affects the person(s) whom discrimination is perpetrated against, but those harboring racism are as adversely affected as those who are victims of this type of hatred. Some are struggling with anger, resentment, and bitterness due to the poisonous venom of racism. If you have been a perpetrator of racism then you're harboring anger, resentment, and bitterness. Victims of racism may well become racist themselves. If those who have been victims of racism allows that action to influence their behavior by being angry, resentful, bitter, and harboring an unforgiving spirit toward those who have perpetrated racism against them, then struggles of life becomes too overwhelming to overcome. There are several emotional disorders that may develop as a result of bitterness and an unforgiving spirit: Anti-Social behavior, Passive Aggressive behavior, Paranoia, and other disorders may affect individuals. Is there any question as to why people cannot overcome everyday struggles in life? As pointed out in chapter 1, Dr. John Babbler, a professor at Southwestern Baptist Theological Seminary in Fort Worth, Texas, during spring of 1999 made this statement in a class entitled "Counseling with Scripture." "Whenever someone with depression comes to me for counseling, I know if I dig deep enough that I will find sin at the root of the problem."[138]

---

[136] Gen. 39:9.

[137] Prov. 22:1.

[138] Babler, 1999.

Do you really want to get the monkey off your back? Why not follow Joseph's example and do the right thing, regardless of what that may mean in your past or current situation. Just do the right thing. Are you asking "what is the right thing?" It is not what your closest friend(s) may tell you unless it lines up with the Word of God. "He has shown you, O man, what is good; and what does the Lord require of you but to do **justly**, to **love mercy**, And to **walk humbly** with your God?[139] Why don't you do what the Lord tells you to do? Stop asking people what you should do and just follow the Word of God. The solution to your problem is right before your eyes. Now you can get the proverbial monkey off your back. For anyone who chooses to do the right thing, it must be ushered in by forgiveness. All of the answers or solutions to your problems are girded by forgiveness. Remember, "And whenever you stand praying, If you have anything against anyone, forgive him, that your Father in heaven may also forgive you your trespasses. But if you do not forgive, neither will your Father in heaven forgive your trespasses."[140] You have done some things in your life that had to be brought before a loving God. God had to forgive you for those things before you could really move on with living your life. You too must be willing to forgive others who may have offended, hurt, or harmed you in any way. More importantly, there are those who perhaps have such a tremendously difficult time forgiving themselves. Often people are their own worst enemy. If you really want to get the monkey off your back, you must be willing to forgive yourself.

Forgiveness Restores Fellowship

In the first epistle of John the subject matter is all about fellowship. John instructs Believers how to restore right fellowship with the Godhead. "If we confess our sins, He is faithful and just to forgive us our sins and to cleanse us from all unrighteousness."[141] Here John demonstrates the essence of forgiveness by telling Believers that if they will confess and repent of their sin(s), that God will not only forgive them but will also erase the stain of unrighteousness. The word confess

---

[139] Mic. 6:8.
[140] Mark 11:25-26.
[141] 1 Jn. 1:9.

in this passage in the original language (Greek) is the word ***homologeo***, which means to acknowledge or agree with God that He is right and you are wrong. Unfortunately this passage (**1 John 1:9**) is for Believers only not Unbelievers, and any attempt to turn it into some "***soteriological*** [salvation] affirmation is misguided"[142] The passage simply restores broken fellowship with God, but no one can be in right fellowship with God if they are not in right fellowship with other Believers.

> This is the message which we have heard from Him and declare to you, that God is light and in Him is no darkness at all. If we say that we have fellowship with Him, and walk in darkness, we lie and do not practice the truth. But if we walk in the light as He is in the light, we have fellowship with one another, and the blood of Jesus Christ His Son cleanses us from all sin."[143]

According to Walvoord and Zuck, each Believer is responsible to "acknowledge (the meaning of "confess," ***homologomen***; cf. [1 John] 2:23; 4:3) whatever the light makes [him/her] aware of, and when [he/she] does so, a complete and perfect cleansing is granted [him/her]."[144] There is one thing for certain in the process of restoring right fellowship with God, Believers must also be in right fellowship with one another. Someone is asking the question, what if a Believer is willing to restore right fellowship with another Believer and the other person refuses to do so? The answer may be as simple as having a willing heart.

"Take heed to yourselves, If your brother sins against you, rebuke him, and if he repents, forgive him. And if he sins against you seven times in a day, and seven times in a day returns to you saying, I repent, you shall forgive him."[145]

According to the scribes, no one has the power to forgive sin except God.[146] Yet when Jesus was teaching the Disciples how to pray He said pray like this:

---

[142] Bible Knowledge Commentary N.T. s.v. "soteriological" (886).

[143] 1 Jn. 1:5-7.

[144] Ibid. s.v. "confess" (886).

[145] Luke 17:3-4.

[146] Mk. 2:7b

> Our Father in heaven, Hallowed be Your name. Your kingdom come. Your will be done On Earth as it is in heaven. Give us this day our daily bread, And forgive us our debts, As we forgive our debtors. And do not lead us into temptation, But deliver us from the evil one. For Yours is the kingdom and the power and the glory forever. Amen.[147]

The purpose for introducing the "Model Prayer" sometimes referred to as the Lord's Prayer, is to place significant attention upon the part of the prayer where the person praying ask God to forgive them their debts as they forgive others their debts. This is a profound rendering since it appears by human reasoning that the individual praying is making a statement that God should forgive them only if they are willing to forgive others. Prayer consisting of confession and repentance leads to Forgiveness. Forgiveness leads to right Fellowship; moreover, whether it is God doing the Forgiving or it is people willing to Forgive, Believers should always be willing to Forgive no matter what the circumstances. Earlier in this chapter it was pointed out how devastating harboring an unforgiving spirit can be. Do not allow an unforgiving spirit to destroy you. Now this is what "getting the monkey off your back" is all about.

---

[147] Matt. 6:9b-13.

CHAPTER 5

Called To Serve

Called for a Purpose

Now you are prepared to serve in the most effective means possible, because God can use someone who recognizes their frailties, character defects, and short-comings more effectively than someone who thinks he/she has it all together. When God calls lost sinners out of the world into the body of Christ, He calls everyone to specific areas of service. Deliverance is maintained by involvement in service to others. Since God does not need anything from people, the only genuine way to serve Him is by serving other people. Service keeps one connected to the process of recovery and restoration, since he/she continues to revisit the principles as they share them with others.

Unfortunately there are those who would rather sit back and watch others do all of the serving and be the recipients of that service. In most cases these Believers seem to be stunted in spiritual growth and may not handle adversity as well as those who are actively involved in Christian service. It is through service that Believers begin to grow and become over-comers in this world. Boice tells of a young man that wrote asking him advice on how he could remain strong in his Christian faith during the period of time he would spend in college. He was from the mid-west and just happened to be in his first year at Howard University. He was concerned about the pressure and dominance of the secular viewpoint and how that would impose upon his values. Boice advised the young man to do three things:

> A period of daily Bible study and prayer; (2) regular fellowship and worship with other Christians, both with his peers (perhaps in a Dorm Bible study or in some other student meeting of Christians) and in a weekly church service and (3) some form of regular service to others. I suggested that this last point could take many forms: an outreach to non-Christians, a tutoring project for the disadvantaged or Social Service work, for example. Only in such activity do we get our minds off ourselves and onto others and their problems, as Christ indicated we should do if we are to be His disciples.[148]

It is very clear in scripture that God has called every Believer in Christ to service, i.e. ministry.

> There are diversities of gifts, but the same Spirit. There are differences of ministries, but the same Lord. But one and the same Spirit works all these things, distributing to each one individually as He wills.[149] And He Himself gave some to be apostles, some prophets, some evangelists, and some pastors and teachers, for the equipping of the saints for the work of ministry, for the edifying of the body of Christ . . . [150]

Called to Ministry

When a Believer does not participate in ministry by acts of service it stunts the growth of that individual as well as the body of Christ and creates a burden.

"From whom the whole body joined and knit together by what every joint supplies, according to the effective working by which every part does its share, causes growth of the body for the edifying of itself in love."[151]

As the Believer goes about serving it opens the door to share the love of Jesus Christ with others. If a man is hungry it is unlikely that

---

[148]   Boice 1986, 500.

[149]   1 Cor. 12:4,5,11.

[150]   Eph. 4:11-12.

[151]   Eph. 4:16.

he would pay attention to what someone is attempting to share with him until that individual provides food for that man's physical body. Ministering or serving is really meeting some type of need. Ministry Based Evangelism is such an effective tool for this reason alone. If people are going to receive the message of the Gospel, there must be the fulfillment of a need. The Evangelist must present the candidate with a reasonable scenario, using scripture as the foundation for his/her argument; moreover, proving that anyone functioning apart from the mercy and grace of God is destined for eternal separation from Him. To do this one must be able to get the candidate's attention. This can be done sometimes just by sharing a personal testimony, a scripture concerning judgment, or the requirements to enter the kingdom of heaven. Not every Believer in Christ is a gifted evangelist, but every Believer in Christ is called to evangelize. Not every Believer in Christ is a gifted teacher, but every Believer in Christ is called to teach God's word.

Called to Glorify God

"Let your light so shine before men, that they may see your good works and glorify your Father in heaven."[152]

Often people are more concerned about getting the glory for themselves rather than bringing glory to God. While claiming they are doing things to glorify God, they really want a little of that glory for themselves. In the Gospel of Matthew chapter 20 there was a mother who no doubt thought the world of her sons and she approached the Lord Jesus about her sons sitting in the place of honor on either side of Jesus in His Kingdom. The father of these two boys was Zebedee and the names of the boys were James and John. Now these two boys had a zeal for God and were somewhat of a daring duo. They were given the name "sons of thunder" to characterize their radical approach to representing their God. They did not approach Jesus but their mother did on their behalf. Then Jesus proceeded by asking the boys if they could drink the cup that He was about to drink, and if they could be baptized with the baptism that He was about to experience, and they

---

[152] Matt. 5:16.

answered "we are able."[153] Jesus explained that they would indeed drink His cup, and be baptized with His baptism. He informed them that to sit at His right hand and left hand was not His to grant, instead God the Father would determine who would be entitled to sit in these places of honor. When the ten disciples heard about the request made by the boys' mother, they became indignant. Jesus called them all to Himself and began explaining what it really meant to be great, because they were competing for position. This is the problem with people who want glory for themselves. There is the desire for one-up-shipmen between peers, so that there is a constant struggle and vying for power. This type of attitude does not project a Christ-centered mentality, but it demonstrates and depicts a self-centered mind-set. Jesus went on to teach them what it really mean to be great.

> You know that the rulers of the Gentiles lord it over them, and those who are great exercise authority over them. Yet it shall not be so among you; but whoever desires to become great among you, let him be your servant. And whoever desires to be first among you, let him be your slave just as the Son of Man did not come to be served, but to serve, and to give His life a ransom for many.[154]

Spiritual Gifts for Service

God has given gifts to every Believer in Christ for the benefit of others and not for themselves.

"But the manifestation of the Spirit is given to each one for the profit of all."[155] The special abilities or spiritual gifts are given that the Believer may be equipped to offer divine service, first to the Body of Christ, which is the Ekklesia[156] or 'Called out Ones.' These are those who make up the church. The church is not a place but a group of people sharing a united belief in the Lord Jesus Christ. The gifted Believer is also responsible for doing divine service unto the Unbeliever

---

[153] Ibid. 20:22.
[154] Matt. 20:25-28.
[155] 1 Cor. 12:7.
[156] Strong's Greek Dictionary s.v. "Church" (1577).

as well. The only way for Unbelievers to be introduced to Christ is through acts of divine service rendered by Believers. While the church teaches that we are to become servants of God, the truth is that God really does not need anyone's service. The only way that anyone can truly serve God is by serving other people. God does not have any needs. The opportunity to serve should not be to make a name for one's self. God is not concerned about establishing popularity as much as He is concerned about genuine service. If service is genuine then an individual will not be concerned about being recognized for everything he/she does as acts of service.

"Take heed that you do not do your charitable deeds before men, to be seen by them. Otherwise you have no reward from your Father in heaven."[157] There are various gifts given to the Believers in the body of Christ. No one possesses all the gifts neither can anyone choose his/her gift. Paul mentions gifts in several passages of New Testament Scripture.

> For to one is given the word of wisdom through the Spirit, to another the word of knowledge through the same Spirit, to another faith by the same Spirit, to another gifts of healings by the same Spirit, to another the working of miracles, to another prophecy, to another discerning of spirits, to another different kinds of tongues, to another the interpretation of tongues.[158]

These spiritual gifts are the basic gifts given to every Believer in Christ. Paul goes on to point out to Believers in Rome how the diversity of gifts given to Believers should be utilized.

> Having then gifts differing according to the grace that is given to us, Let us use them: if prophecy, let us prophesy in proportion to our faith; or ministry, let us use it in our ministering; he who teaches, in teaching; he who exhorts, in exhortation; he who gives, with liberality; he who leads, with diligence; he who shows mercy, with cheerfulness.[159]

---

[157]   Matt. 6:1.

[158]   1 Cor. 12:8-10.

[159]   Rom. 12:6-8.

Paul takes spiritual giftedness to another level by telling the reader how Jesus Himself distributed spiritual gifts to men and women for the equipping of the saints for the work of the ministry.

"And He Himself gave some to be apostles, some prophets, some evangelists, and some pastors and teachers, for the equipping of the saints for the work of ministry, for the edifying of the body of Christ . . ."[160]

It is impossible for the Believer to grow unless he/she is involved in ministry. Ministry has everything to do with meeting needs, and sometimes the necessities of life are the needs. Although there are necessities of life, nothing is more important than Unbelievers coming into the saving knowledge of the Lord Jesus Christ. People can serve and not necessarily be in service for the Lord. When one's service is motivated by the Lord or unto the Lord, then that defines the essence of ministry. God does not really need one's service, therefore the only way one can really serve God is by serving people. Believers don't just serve saved people, but they serve those who are lost. Christian service to Unbelievers is the key that opens the door for an invitation to receive the Lord Jesus Christ. The service rendered to Believers and Unbelievers alike is what causes the Christian to grow spiritually. Spiritual growth is necessary for Believers to resist the temptations of Satan and his demons. The old folks use to say that "an idled mind is the devils workshop." This is certainly an old cliché but it is true, and even scripture supports this conclusion.

"I must work the works of Him who sent Me while it is day; the night is coming when no one can work."[161] This previous Scripture quotation recorded in the Gospel of John is the words of the Lord Jesus Christ. If Jesus says that He must work the works of Him who sent Him what are Believers in Christ supposed to be doing? Listen to the exhortation given by Paul the Apostle:

"Let love be without hypocrisy. Abhor what is evil. Cling to what is good. Be kindly affectionate to one another with brotherly love, in honor giving preference to one another; not lagging in diligence, fervent in spirit, serving the Lord . . ."[162] Again the Lord does not

---

[160] Eph. 4:11-12.

[161] Jn. 9:4.

[162] Rom. 12:9-11.

need anyone's service, and the only way one can really serve God is by serving people. How does one determine the area of service God is calling him/her to render? This is not a difficult issue to resolve. If an individual will find an area of interest within the body of Christ, then he/she will learn soon enough if it is something that God is calling him/her to commit to doing on a regular basis. The fact of the matter is that most people wait for someone to tell them what need to be done and then they volunteer for something that God has not gifted them to do, and end up hating their assignment. The brother or sister that have committed to serving will not wait for someone to instruct them in choosing an area of service, but will inquire about particular areas of service and demonstrate desire and ability in the area of service they are seeking. They may also be willing to serve in an area where no one else is willing to be of service.

Labor of Love

Believers serve because they have God's spirit of love. It really is about the love of God and the labor of love that Believers exhibit when reaching out to the world, whether they are lost or saved people. Service must be genuine and the Apostle Paul pointed this out in the scripture quotation listed earlier.

"Let love be without hypocrisy,"[163] and service is the Believer's way of extending the love of God to those who are in need. Sometimes the need is salvation and other times it may be felt needs or the necessities of life. Nevertheless, service is meeting needs and giving support that may include but is not limited to prayer, moral support, fellowship, worship, discipleship, and instruction in righteousness.

> Our calling is to exhibit the existence of God and to exhibit his character, Individually and collectively. God is holy and God is love, and our calling is simultaneously to show forth holiness and love in every aspect of life—as parent and child, as husband and wife, in business, in our Christian organizations, in the church, in government, in everything—an exhibition of the character of God showing forth his holiness and his love

---

[163] Rom. 12:9a NKJV.

> simultaneously. If we depend on the flesh rather than the work of the Spirit, it is easy to say we are showing holiness and yet it is only egotistic pride and hardness. Equally, in the flesh rather than the work of the Spirit, it is easy to say we are showing forth love and it is only egotistic compromise, latitudinarianism, and accommodation. Both are equally easy in the flesh. Both are equally egotistic. To show forth both simultaneously, in personal matters or in church and public life, can only be done in any real degree by our consciously bowing, denying our egotistic selves, and letting Christ bring forth his fruit through us—not merely as a "religious" statement, but with some ongoing reality.[164]

If the Believer is genuine in their estimation of service then he/she will recognize that service produces fruit. If no fruit is being produced then service is not really going forth. Jesus made this statement in the Gospel of Saint John:

"You did not choose Me, but I chose you and appointed you that you should go and bear fruit, and that your fruit should remain, that whatever you ask the Father in My name He may give you. These things I command you, that you love one another."[165] If anyone really wants to be an over-comer he/she must become a servant of Christ, and of course it has been pointed out in this chapter that one cannot really serve God unless he/she serves people. God does not really need any service from anyone, since He is self sufficient. If anyone really want to get the monkey off of their back they only need to be obedient and begin serving and contributing to the work of the ministry, and God will work miracles in the circumstances concerning their life.

> Servants, be obedient to them that are your masters according to the flesh, with fear and trembling, in singleness of your heart, as unto Christ; Not with eyeservice, as men-pleasers; but as the servants of Christ, doing the will of God from the heart; With good will doing service, as to the Lord, and not to men:

---

[164] Schaeffer 1983 75-76.
[165] John 15:16-17 NKJV.

Knowing that whatsoever good thing any man doeth, the same
shall he receive of the Lord, whether he be bond or free.[166]

How does one really serve God by serving other people? Listen to
the words of this scholar concerning divine service:

> It is easier to serve ourselves, of course. But we must not. First,
> the presence of good works in a Christian's life is one evidence
> of salvation. We now think differently than we did before our
> conversion and seek to serve others in ways that would never
> have occurred to us before. Here is evidence that we are new
> creatures in Christ. Second, doing good works is a means of
> growth in the Christian life. If we desire this, we should serve
> others faithfully. What happens if we do not? We become
> introverted selfish, insensitive and mean. When we do good to
> others our horizons are broadened, we grow in soul and become
> more and more like Jesus. Third, (and how self-evident), good
> works are a blessing to those we serve. It is hard to put ourselves
> in the place of others, particularly when they are needy and we
> are well off. But it will help us in this regard to remember that
> service to others is service to our Lord. "Then the King will
> say to those at his right hand, 'Come, O blessed of my Father,
> inherit the kingdom prepared for you from the foundation of
> the world; for I was hungry and you gave me food, I was thirsty
> and you gave me drink, I was a stranger and you welcomed me.
> I was naked and you clothed me, I was sick and you visited me,
> I was in prison and you came to me'" (Mt. 25:34-36). Jesus is
> blessed through our service to others; and if he is, so are they.
> Finally, God is glorified by our works. Only through his life
> within and by his grace are we able to do them.[167]

Service is the key to personal growth, the growth of others, and
the kingdom work that will fulfill the kingdom agenda. What is the
kingdom agenda? Peter seems to have recorded it plain and clear in the
following passage:

---

[166]   Eph. 6:5-8 KJV.
[167]   Boice 1986, 506.

"The Lord is not slack concerning his promise, as some men count slackness; but is long suffering toward us, not willing that any should perish, but that all should come to repentance."[168]

Anyone can get the monkey off their back if they will surrender their lives to the Lord Jesus Christ and surrender what they think they know and what they think they can do. If they respond to the instructions given concerning worship and praise. If they are obedient to their call to ministry by serving the Lord and others, then anyone can be victorious in over-coming strongholds. Service is not an option it is necessary for genuine Christian growth.

---

[168] 2 Pet. 3:9 KJV.

CHAPTER 6

Carrying The Message

Messenger of Recovery

In the first two chapters the reader was able to identify the 'Problem' and 'Solution' to the struggles that ensue when there is a monkey on one's back. Getting the monkey off your back requires a process of recovery that impacts every area of an individual's life. What does one do to maintain consistent adherence to the principles of recovery, after finally he/she has successfully gotten the monkey off their back? This question will be answered in the three concluding chapters of this book. Consider the close association between the 12th Step of Alcoholics Anonymous, and the divine statements and instructions of the Bible:

"Having had a spiritual awakening as the result of these steps, we tried to carry this message to alcoholics, and to practice these principles in all our affairs."[169]

> "Go therefore and make disciples of all the nations, baptizing them in the name of the Father, and of the Son, and of the Holy Spirit, teaching them to observe all things that I have commanded you; and lo, I am with you always, even to the end of the age." Amen.[170]

---

[169] Alcoholics Anonymous 1976, 60.

[170] Matt. 28:19-20 NKJV.

As the observation of the distinct message of the two sources occurs, consider how the nature of both reveal God's divine plan for constant reconciliation and training in the kingdom agenda. First, the book of Alcoholics Anonymous specifies that after one experiences spiritual birth, then he/she carries the message to those who are still dead spiritually. It is the spirit life, and this must be qualified in the fact that the Spirit of God must be the source of spiritual influence awakening the spiritually dead.

"And you He made alive, who were dead in trespasses and sins."[171] According to both sources there is a didactic element that is also commanded and necessary for the growth of both the messenger and the recipient of the message. In the 12th Step as noted above, the messenger as well as the recipient of the message are instructed to practice certain principles in all their affairs. There is no variation to this imperative when observing the word of the Lord Jesus Christ contained in the passage quoted above. He tells the messenger and the recipients as they are teaching those whom they come into contact with the ways of discipleship, the teacher should be careful to observe all the things that Jesus, the master teacher has commanded them. He goes on to say that He will be with the messenger and the recipient of the message always; even to the end of the world. Amen.

Sponsorship vs. Discipleship

In the 12 Step recovery programs those who carry the message are generally referred to as Sponsors. Sponsors offer support and guidance to the Newcomers of the 12 Step programs. In biblical terms, the Newcomer is described as the New Convert or Novice.[172] Sponsors take the Newcomer through the principles and processes of recovery as well as offer support and resources. The resources may include but is not limited to rides to meetings, the necessities of life, pointing out character defects and flaws, as well as giving moral and spiritual support. Discipleship is similar to Sponsorship in that the Disciple maker teaches the Disciple the word of God, models the Christian lifestyle, provides resources for the Disciple, and encourages the Disciple morally and

---

[171] Eph. 2:1 NKJV.
[172] 1 Tim. 3:6 KJV.

spiritually. Both of the recipients are students in constant training that becomes a life-long process. Discipleship and Sponsorship is also a life-long commitment that keeps both the Disciple maker and the Sponsor on a beaten path.

The Gospel Message

The gospel of Mark begins by introducing John the Baptizer as the one spoken of by the prophets,[173] who prophesied concerning the arrival of the Lord. Mark identified this individual as the Messenger of the Lord. Some scholars refer to him as the fore- runner that brings the "good news" or what is referred to as the Gospel.

> Behold, I send My messenger before Your face, Who will prepare Your way before You. The voice of one crying in the wilderness: Prepare the way of the Lord; Make His paths straight. John came baptizing in the wilderness and preaching a baptism of repentance for the remission of sins.[174] "I indeed baptized you with water but He will baptize you with the Holy Spirit." Now after John was put In prison, Jesus came to Galilee, preaching the gospel of the kingdom of God, and saying "The time is fulfilled, and the kingdom of God is at hand, Repent, and believe in the gospel.[175]

As Mark's gospel was coming to a close he records this command given by the Lord Jesus Christ. "And He said to them, "Go into all the world and preach the gospel to every creature. "He who believes and is baptized will be saved; but he who does not believe will be condemned."[176] Every Believer is given the command to carry the gospel message to everyone they come into contact with. Carrying the gospel message is not optional, it is a command given by the Lord Jesus Christ Himself. If one believes that faith in Christ and eternal life is genuinely the greatest thing anyone alive could possess, those possessing such

---

[173]   Isa. 40:3.

[174]   Mark 1:2-4.

[175]   Ibid. 1:8,14,15.

[176]   Mark 16:15-16.

a gift will not keep it to themselves. Many who have made a verbal confession but not a genuine confession don't share the gospel because they really have not experienced regeneration. They have not genuinely experienced the transformation that comes through Christ and His extension of eternal life to those who believe in His name.

"These things I have written to you who believe in the name of the Son of God, that you may know that you have eternal life, and that you may continue to believe in the name of the Son of God"[177] Some have asked the question, how can one truly know that they have eternal life? The answer is given in the previous scripture quotation. There is a way that one can know for sure that he/she has eternal life. Certainly if one believes that Heaven exist they must believe that Hell exist as well. No one in right standing with God wants anyone to deny Heaven exist and end up in Hell. Therefore if one has a genuine relationship with Jesus Christ they will share what they have, because it is too serious to keep to themselves.

Believers as Recruiters

Believers have a responsibility for ministering to the body of Christ, and they are also called to recruit Unbelievers and enlist them into God's program of Discipleship.

> Go therefore and make disciples of all the nations, baptizing them in the name of the Father and of the Son and of the Holy Spirit, "teaching them to observe all things that I have commanded you; and lo, I am with you always, even to the end of the age. Amen.[178]

Proper exegesis is in order for the previous scripture quotation that the reader may have a deeper understanding as to the responsibility of every Believer in Christ. Many have made a confession for the Lord Jesus Christ, but unfortunately have not entered into the process of discipleship. The word Disciple in the original language (Greek) is the

---

[177] 1 Jn. 5:13.
[178] Matt. 28:19-20.

word **matheteuo**[179] and denotes one who becomes a literal learner, i.e. pupil. The word 'nations' is the word **ethnos**,[180] which is where the English word ethnic is derived. Therefore Believers are commanded to break racial barriers by carrying this message to every ethnic group. The singular connotation of the Godhead, "in the name of the Father and of the Son and of the Holy Spirit . . . ," denotes the co-equality of these three distinct persons. They are co-equal in knowledge, power, and presence. The word 'teaching' in verse 20 unlike the word 'teach' in verse 19 is the word **didasko**. From **dao** (to learn); to teach (in the same broad application); Teach suggests that one teaches as he/she learns.[181] Remember the word 'teach' [KJV] in verse 19 is the word Disciple and the word 'teaching' in verse 20 is referring to one that teaches as he/she learns. As Believers carry the message of the Gospel they may not realize that every time they share the message there is a blessing in it for them as well. "So then faith comes by hearing and hearing by the word of God"[182] Paul tells the Believer that faith is a development that comes as a result of hearing God's word. What a powerful revelation to experience for one who is consistently sharing their faith with other people. They are not sharing their faith with other people for what they can get out of it, but what a tremendous realization for the Believer to know that as they are sharing with others they are also hearing God's word and being blessed as their faith increases. Of course faith is also increased by experiencing adversity. "My brethren, count it all joy when you fall into various trials, knowing that the testing of your faith produces patience."[183] The realization is that people can overcome trials, tribulations, and strongholds by reaching out to others through the sharing of the Gospel message. In essence this is another piece of the puzzle involving service that will aid you in getting the monkey off your back. God will give you divine appointments and through these divine appointments many will come to Christ through your obedience to share the Gospel, and as a result you will recruit many for discipleship and find that the strongholds in your life are being pulled down.

---

[179] Strong's Greek Dictionary s.v. "teach [disciple]" (3100).

[180] Ibid. s.v. "ethnos" (1484).

[181] Ibid. s.v. "teaching" (1321).

[182] Rom. 10:17.

[183] Js. 1:2-3.

J. Emil Terry

The Legitimate Witness

Most people are apprehensive when it comes to sharing their faith. If anyone is living a Christ-like lifestyle they should not be hesitant to share their faith with others. If what the Believer has in Christ is really the most significant commodity in the present life and the one to come, then he/she should want everyone to know about this magnificent development that has occurred in their life. For example when women find a great product that enhances their beauty, whether it is a hair or cosmetic item they will generally get on the phone and tell friends, family, and co-workers about this great product they have discovered. In essence the manufacturer is depending on a percentage of purchasers to promote their products by word of mouth through results they get from using the item(s). In the same way if Jesus Christ is the best thing that ever happened to humanity, then every Believer in Christ should be telling everyone he/she meets about this marvelous Savior. If anyone is genuinely going to receive your message concerning Jesus Christ and His greatness, then it will be as a result of the lifestyle you are living. Often people want to tell others that they need Jesus, but cannot really tell them why they need Him. Others are attempting to tell people how miraculously Jesus has worked in their lives but they are still living like lost people. It is possible to effectively witness to others when one's life is not completely lining up with God's word, but those that know you will be more responsive when they witness your godly lifestyle. The Apostle Paul had this exhortation to offer the churches in Asia Minor:

> I therefore, the prisoner of the Lord, beseech you to walk worthy of the calling with which you were called, with all lowliness and gentleness, with longsuffering, bearing with one another in love, endeavoring to keep the unity of the spirit in the bond of peace. There is one body and one Spirit, just as you were called in one hope of your calling; one Lord, one faith, one baptism, one God and Father of all, who is above all, and through all, and in you all.[184]

---

[184] Eph. 4:1-4.

The Apostle Paul is pleading with Believers to join him in living a Christ-like lifestyle. When he says "I beseech you . . . ." the beseech in the original language (Greek) is the word *parakaleo*,[185] which denotes one calling someone else to join in with them. It is a literal plea of exhortation to the one whom is being called. Paul makes it clear that first one must be willing to "walk worthy . . . ." The word walk in this passage does not refer to advancing by steps, instead it refers to one's lifestyle or manner of life. The word in the original language (Greek) is *peripateo*,[186] a figurative term denoting the activities surrounding the life of those whether they are Believers or not. The word worthy in the original language (Greek) is *axios*,[187] which means of equal measure. This term puts one in the mind of trading or buying and selling. During the era that Paul lived and ministered, people used double sided scales to buy, sale, and trade. There were times when the person selling would pad the scale or cheat in weighing product and the purchaser was under the impression that he/she was getting what they traded for, when in reality they were being cheated. Therefore when the Apostle Paul exhorts Believers to "walk worthy" he is really making a statement that Believers' lives are suppose to line up with their witness or testimony about who they are and whose they are. In essence let your walk match your talk, or practice what you preach. If you say you are a Believer then your lifestyle should make the same statement. The Believer should not talk, walk, act, or conduct themselves as those who are unsaved or worldly. Unsaved and worldly really mean the same thing. It just means that they are not Believers in Christ, and a Believer in Christ has eternal life as we saw in an earlier quote from 1 John 5:13. After the Apostle Paul pleads with Believers to live a Christ-like lifestyle, He then tells them how to carry out such a difficult task. First, he tells them to do it "with all lowliness." The word *Tapeinophrosune*[188] (Greek) means that they are to do it with humiliation in mind. The Believer can only do what the Apostle Paul is suggesting if he/she is humble or modest in spirit. Second, he tells them that they must do it with gentleness. This term from the word

---

[185] Strong's Greek Dictionary s.v. "parakaleo" (3870).

[186] Ibid. s.v. "peripateo" (4043).

[187] Ibid. s.v. "axios" (516).

[188] Ibid. s.v. "lowliness" (5012).

Prautetos[189] is where the word meek derives from and most people are confuse with the meaning of the word meek. Somehow people draw the conclusion that meek means weak, and nothing could be further from the truth. Meek actually speaks to one having the ability to exercise power, but withholds the right to do so. For example when Jesus was on the Cross at Calvary He could have called down a legion of angels to wipe out His enemies, but He withheld the power to do so. Therefore a good definition for the word meek perhaps is power under control. One may have the power to respond to a situation and yet does not exercise that power, but holds back even when they have the authority or the right to do so. Third, the Apostle Paul tells them to be longsuffering. The word ***Makrothymia***[190] (Greek) means forbearance or patience. He is really telling Believers they should be willing to put up with one another regardless of their character flaws or short comings. Fourth, he is telling them to bear with one another in love. The word bearing or forbearing (KJV) is the word ***Anecho***[191] (Greek)—***ana*** means up, and ***echo*** to have or hold; to bear with or endure or to bear up under. It puts one in the mind of an Ant that is working hard to gather goods for survival. Often the Ant though very small will be carrying something very large. It is astonishing to see the Ant carrying something that is larger than the creature itself. When considering the exhortation given by the Apostle Paul, one might question why anyone would want to work so hard and carry such a large burden on their backs? When Believers consider the goodness of God and His loving kindness toward them, then they have no problem sharing that same loving kindness toward other people. The Apostle Paul goes on to give the final analysis for carrying out this exhortation. He tells the Believer that the result will be "endeavoring to keep the unity of the Spirit in the bond of peace."[192] This means that the Believer is being persistent in keeping unity among Believers through the Spirit of God to promote bonding that will foster peace. He goes on to point out that every Believer has been called by the same Lord and Father for the same purpose although their giftedness and function may vary.

---

[189] Ibid. s.v. "meekness" (4236).
[190] Ibid. s.v. "longsuffering" (3115).
[191] Ibid. s.v. "bearing/forbearing" (430).
[192] Eph. 4:3.

When carrying the message effectively, one should demonstrate godly character and Christ-like qualities if he/she hopes to be effective as they witness. Very rarely does anyone experience spiritual growth until they begin experiencing and practicing the principles contained in God's word. Do you really want to get the monkey off your back? Don't just carry the message but allow the message to be your lifestyle, then you can get the monkey off your back.

CHAPTER 7

Accountability

Role and Responsibility

What is accountability, and what does it mean to be accountable? Webster defines accountability in this way: 1) Subject to giving an account: Answerable 2) Capable of being accounted for: Explainable: *syn* see Responsible—accountability.[193] Dr. James Montgomery Boice gives an intriguing revelation to his readers concerning accountability. Listen to what he says to the reader:

> Most of what has been said up to this point has been encouraging, particularly for Christians, but there is a sober side too. Christ is coming. His coming will be a joy for Christians, who will be raised to meet him. But it will also mean the beginning of Christ's judgments for those who have spurned the gospel. Christians acknowledge this truth every time they recite the Apostles' Creed. The say Jesus will come again from heaven "to judge the living and the dead." The Victorian poet Robert Browning wrote, "God's in his heaven; all's right with the world." But although God is in his heaven, all is not right with the world, and a day is coming when God will speak out against the world in judgment. Paul told the Athenians that God "has fixed a day on which he will judge the world in

---

[193] Webster s.v. "accountable" (50).

righteousness by a man whom he has appointed, and of this he has given assurance to all men by raising him from the dead" (Acts 17:31). That is a sobering fact. It tells us that history has an end, and its end involves accountability. We shall answer for what we have done, and we shall all be judged either on the basis of our own righteousness (which will condemn us) or on the basis of the perfect righteousness of him who is our Savior. Some people refuse to face this reality and go on ignoring the day of reckoning.[194]

Reaching the Unbeliever

Every Believer is called into service by the Lord Jesus Christ and is automatically given a specific role and has specific responsibilities appointed by God. The information and instructions of this literature continually refers to the Believer, but of course the principles will work for anyone that applies them. However, if anyone applies the principles embodied in this literature, they will no longer be an Unbeliever. Practicing these principles will lead to a conversion experience and the revelation of God will be the result. Four aspects that must be clarified before moving ahead in this chapter: First, defining conversion; Second, the association between conversion and the Believer's role; Third, the revelation of God and what that means to every Believer; Finally, the responsibility that proceeds conversion and how the Believer exercises their 'Role and Responsibility' before their fellow man and God. First, conversion refers to the process that occurs when one comes into a personal or intimate relationship with Jesus Christ. The Bible refers to this process as salvation and clearly point out that salvation comes through the establishment of a relationship with Jesus Christ.

"The word is near you, in your mouth and in your heart" (that is, the word of faith which we preach): that if you confess with your mouth the Lord Jesus and believe in your heart that God has raised Him from the dead, you will be saved. For with the

---

[194]   Boice 1986, 711-712.

heart one believes unto righteousness, and with the mouth confession is made unto salvation.[195]

According to Strong's, the word "confess" in the previous quote in the original language of Greek (*Homologeho*) is defined "to assent, i.e. covenant, acknowledge."[196] In the context of the passage quoted, it implies that one is agreeing with God about all that is contained in the passage. The agreement implies that Jesus is Lord over all creation whether someone wants Him to be or not. Also that God the Father raised Him from the dead whether people believe it or not. Furthermore, that God is right and all of mankind is wrong.

> What advantage then has the Jew, or what is the profit of circumcision? Much in every way! Chiefly because to them were committed the oracles of God. For what if some did not believe? Will their unbelief make the faithfulness of God without effect? Certainly not! Indeed, let God be true but every man a liar. As it is written: "That You may be justified in Your words, And may overcome when You are judged."[197]

Only One Way to God

The previous quote strengthens the implication of Romans 10:8-10, confirming that those who come into a personal or intimate relationship with God through Jesus Christ must acknowledge their wrong and realize that God is always right, and this is what faith is really about. Trusting God for being all that He says about Himself is the genuine essence of faith. The question arises as to how an individual reaches the point of making the confession for Jesus Christ to begin with? Well, the Holy Spirit is the agent of regeneration and the dead soul or the person without Christ is spiritually dead. "And you He made alive, who were dead in trespasses and sins, . . ."[198] The person referred to as "He" would be the Holy Spirit who is the agent of regeneration.

---

[195]   Rom. 10:8-10.

[196]   Strong's Greek Dictionary s.v. "confess/homologeho" (52).

[197]   Rom. 3:1-4.

[198]   Eph. 2:1.

The reason the term regeneration is used clarifies the necessity for one to be recreated. This recreation comes through divine transformation. "Therefore, if anyone is in Christ, he is a new creation; old things have passed away; behold, all things have become new."[199]

There is another factor involved in the process of salvation. There is no other way of acquiring salvation nor is there any other source by which salvation is attainable. Jesus Christ is the only way of attaining salvation. "Jesus said to him, I am the way, the truth, and the life. No one comes to the Father except through Me."[200] "Nor is there salvation in any other, for there is no other name under heaven given among men by which we must be saved."[201] Concerning the word saved and its etymology, this definition is given from the original language since the New Testament is originally written in Greek. According to Strong, the word 'saved' in the Greek is the word *Sozo* and the phonetics for proper pronunciation Sode'-zo means "safe, i.e. deliver or protect (lit. or fig.):—heal, preserve, save (self), do well, be (make) whole."[202]

Authenticity of Scripture

If anyone believes the veracity, inerrancy, and the infallibility of scripture, the preceding quotes from scripture should be enough to convince the greatest critics and skeptics that there is only one way to God the Father. Second, the association between conversion and the Believer's role deals with what should occur after one comes into a personal or intimate relationship with the Lord Jesus Christ. There is a story in the Bible about a man who supposedly lived according to the law of God. This man's name was Saul, not to be confused with the first king of Israel. This man went about the business on a daily basis of taking Believers into custody and incarcerating, torturing, tormenting, and even putting them to death, because of tradition. His assaults on mankind and his conversion story can be found in the book entitled "The Acts of the Apostles," in chapters 7-9, 22-28 of the Holy Bible.

---

[199] 2 Cor. 5:17.

[200] John 14:6.

[201] Acts 4:12.

[202] Strong's Greek Dictionary s.v. "save/sozo" (70).

When discussing the Believer's conversion and role there are at least three factors involved:

A) Total surrender is necessary if we expect God to provide protection and eternal security.
B) God does not save us just for the purpose of keeping us safe from harm, but expect us to reach out to others.
C) Believers are responsible for living holy lifestyles.

While the scope of these three factors covers such a broad spectrum, it is not possible to list all the things involved that would apply to the role and responsibility of Believers. However, understanding that God requires Believers to surrender, reach out to others, and live holy lifestyles gives a primary explanation of what pleases God. Concerning 'surrender' Dr. Luke recorded this exhortation given by Jesus Christ Himself:

> Then He said to them all, "If anyone desires to come after Me, let him deny himself, and take up his cross daily, and follow Me. For whoever desires to save his life will lose it, but whoever loses his life for My sake will save it. For what profit is it to a man if he gains the whole world, and is himself destroyed or lost? . . ."[203]

Concerning reaching out to others Saint Matthew records this exhortation given by Jesus Christ Himself:

> All authority has been given to Me in heaven and on earth. Go therefore and make disciples of all the nations, baptizing them in the name of the Father and of the Son and of the Holy Spirit, teaching them to observe all things that I have commanded you; and lo, I am with you always, even to the end of the age. Amen.[204]

---

[203] Luke 9:23-25.
[204] Matt. 28:19-20.

J. Emil Terry

Concerning living a holy lifestyle the Apostle Paul gives this exhortation:

> Therefore be imitators of God as dear children. And walk in love, as Christ also has loved us and given Himself for us, an offering and a sacrifice to God for a sweet-smelling aroma. But fornication and all uncleanness or covetousness, let it not even be named among you, as is fitting for saints; neither filthiness, nor foolish talking, nor coarse jesting, which are not fitting, but rather giving of thanks. For this you know, that no fornicator, unclean person, nor covetous man, who is an idolater, has any inheritance in the kingdom of Christ and God. Let no one deceive you with empty words, for because of these things the wrath of God comes upon the sons of disobedience. Therefore do not be partakers with them.[205]

What Should Follow Conversion

For clear illustrations of what the previous three factors involves, Saul's story will define and describe each of these factors in detail. In relationship to total surrender in the 'A' factor this exhortation or encouragement is provided:

> Then Saul, still breathing threats and murder against the disciples of the Lord, went to the high priest and asked letters from him to the synagogues of Damascus, so that if he found any who were of the Way, whether men or women, he might bring them bound to Jerusalem. As he journeyed he came near Damascus, and suddenly a light shone around him from heaven. Then he fell to the ground, and heard a voice saying to him, Saul. Saul, why are you persecuting Me?" And he said, "Who are You, Lord?" Then the Lord said, "I am Jesus, whom you are persecuting. It is hard for you to kick against the goads." So he, trembling and astonished, said, "Lord, what do You want me

---

[205] Eph. 5:1-6.

to do." Then the Lord said to him, "Arise and go into the city, and you will be told what you must do."[206]

In this dialogue between the helpless Saul and the Lord total surrender occurs, because at this point Saul was not in a position where he or those who were with him could help in his situation. As a matter of fact it states that those with him at the time "stood speechless, hearing a voice but seeing no one. Then Saul arose from the ground, and when his eyes were opened he saw no one. But they led him by the hand and brought him into Damascus. And he was three days without sight, and neither ate nor drank."[207] The total surrender is demonstrated by Saul conceding to the fact that he was unable to do anything for himself. At this point of surrender he was safe and secure in the protection and eternal security of the Lord. Also, he became willing to do whatever the Lord planned and purposed for his life: "Lord, what do You want me to do?"[208] The **'B'** factor in this conversion experience explains what the Lord would have Saul to do. As the story unfolds there was a man in Damascus named Ananias. Ananias was told "go to the street called Straight, and inquire at the house of Judas for one called Saul of Tarsus, for behold, he is praying."[209] Judas in this particular passage is not to be confused with Judas Iscariot, who betrayed Jesus.[210] At this point Saul is praying for deliverance from his plight of blindness that occurred on the road to Damascus. As Ananias went on his way and finally reached the house where Saul was waiting, he went in and laid hands on Saul. At this point the scripture says that immediately something like scales fell from his eyes and he received his sight.[211] As documented in the passage, Saul received food and was strengthened and after a few days he immediately "preached the Christ in the synagogues, that He is the Son of God."[212]

---

[206] Acts 9:1-6.

[207] Ibid. 9:7-9.

[208] Acts 9:6.

[209] Ibid. 9:11.

[210] Matt. 10:4.

[211] Ibid. 9:17-18.

[212] Ibid. 9:19.

Concerning the 'C' factor and Believers being responsible for living holy lifestyles, which is a tremendous aspect of accountability since every Believer will be held responsible for living right before man and God. The problem associated with living right before mankind is most difficult since people tend to create their own principles for what they believe to be moral and just. There appears to be double standards with most people, and while they may consider their way of life the moral and just way they will point out that which they define as wrong and over-look certain practices that other people would consider wrong. When people follow God's word and just do what it says, then there is no partiality in their assessment of that which is moral and just. Most people that find themselves with a monkey on their backs are responsible for the monkey being on their back. Often people bring misfortune upon themselves and then it takes a miracle to get them out of the circumstances or situations. Barnabas and Saul were appointed by the Holy Spirit to carry the message of the gospel throughout Antioch, Seleucia, Cyprus, Salamis, Paphos, and Pisidia and other cities and providences not yet mentioned. It was at this point that Saul was also referred to as Paul.[213] Over a period of time as Saul/Paul and Barnabas ministered in these cities many created conflict and opposed these two ministers. Elymas the sorcerer attempted to turn the proconsul away from the faith and Saul/Paul rebuked him and he became blind as Saul/Paul witnessed against him.[214] As one follows this turn of events in the life of Saul/Paul, it is clear that he lived a lifestyle of holiness from the time of his conversion on Damascus Road forward. Remember he asked the Lord what he wanted him to do, and Jesus replied it will be told to him what to do. Ananias was reluctant to go as the Lord had directed him to the house of Judas to lay hands on Saul because of Saul's reputation against Believers, but the Lord told Ananias that Saul was a chosen vessel of His. Ananias knew that God was going to hold him accountable for carrying the message of the gospel and reaching out to those who were lost, so Ananias was obedient and did as the Lord had commanded him.

"But the Lord said to him, "Go, for he is a chosen vessel of Mine to bear My name before Gentiles, kings, and the children of Israel.

---

[213] Acts 13:1-13.
[214] Ibid. 13:8-12.

For I will show him how many things he must suffer for My name's sake."[215] As Saul who is now been given a new name to demonstrate a new identity and is called Paul from the Greek **Paulos**, which means to pause, stop, restrain, quit, desist, come to an end, cease, leave or refrain,[216] is relevant to that which occurred when Saul met the Lord on Damascus Road; and Paul during his lifetime sacrificed much to minister to the masses. The Lord certainly did stop Saul in his tracks on the day that he was on his way to Damascus. Needless to say that from that day on Paul ministered in many places to many people and suffered great persecution until his martyrdom. This story is presented to give one the idea of what should occur after conversion becomes reality. If a person truly has a conversion experience and receives the Lord Jesus Christ as their Savior, then factors A, B, and C will be a reality in that person's life as well. There is no way possible that Paul could continue to minister as he did unless he was living a holy lifestyle. Consistently throughout the pages of the Bible and this story about Saul's conversion the word of God is mentioned. Paul received the word directly from the Lord Jesus Christ. After his conversion he carried the message of the word of God everywhere he went. He preached the message of the gospel, which is God's word even from prison in letters sent to various churches he had pioneered.[217] God reveals Himself to humanity through His word. This process of revealing Himself is referred to by scholars as revelation, which leads to the third aspect of experience that the Believer has opportunity to witness.

Revelation of God

Third, the revelation of God and what that means to every Believer: When one goes on a plane ride for the first time and see the landscape from thousands of feet above ground, it may look like some type of pattern that someone has drawn. Some scholars refer to the creation of the heavens and earth as a divine design. Listen to what the Psalmist has to say about the revelation of God.

---

[215] Ibid. 9:15-16.

[216] Strong's Greek Dictionary s.v. "Paul/Paulos" (56).

[217] Eph. 4:1.

J. Emil Terry

> The heavens declare the glory of God; And the firmament shows His handiwork. Day unto day utters speech, And night unto night reveals knowledge. There is no speech nor language Where their voice is not heard. Their line has gone out through all the earth, And their words to the end of the world. In them He has set a tabernacle for the sun, Which is like a bridegroom coming out of his chamber, And rejoices like a strong man to run its race. Its rising is from one end of heaven, And its circuit to the other end; And there is nothing hidden from its heat.[218]

This first part of the Revelation of God in this portion of the Psalms is referred to as Natural or General Revelation. Once again this is God's way of reveling Himself to humanity by what He has created or by what He has made. The scholars may refer to this as God's revelation by divine design. The other part of the Revelation of God is as follows:

> The law of the Lord is perfect, converting the soul; The testimony of the Lord is sure, making wise the simple; The statutes of the Lord are right, rejoicing the heart; The commandment of the Lord is pure, enlightening the eyes; The fear of the Lord is clean, enduring forever; The judgments of the Lord are true and righteous altogether. More to be desired are they than gold, Yea, than much fine gold; Sweeter also than honey and the honeycomb. Moreover by them Your servant is warned, And in keeping them there is great reward. Who can understand his errors? Cleanse me from secret faults. Keep back Your servant also from presumptuous sins; Let them not have dominion over me. Then I shall be blameless, And I shall be innocent of great transgression. Let the words of my mouth and the meditation of my heart Be acceptable in Your sight, O Lord, my Strength and my Redeemer.[219]

This second half of Psalm 19 speak to the reader about the Special Revelation of God. The reason it is referred to as Special Revelation put emphasis on the power of God's word and its regenerating power.

---

[218] Ps. 19:1-6.
[219] Ps. 19:7-14.

In Natural or General Revelation God's handy work is displayed or demonstrated before the entire universe. Natural or General Revelation is just enough information to get humanity in trouble, because after God has revealed Himself to the world everyone must either choose to be with Him or to be against Him. Someone reading this literary work is questioning how God could give people an ultimatum to take sides who have not been formally introduced to Him. Questions asked by people in reference to how people in third world countries who have never seen a Bible, or never had one read to them in their native tongue can possibly know to choose God? How can they choose God if they don't know anything about Him? According to the Apostle Paul, there is an innate principle within mankind that reveals the reality of the divine Creator. Listen to how Paul characterizes this innate factor or principle that deals with the Natural or General Revelation of God:

> For the wrath of God is revealed from heaven against all ungodliness and unrighteousness of men, who suppress the truth in unrighteousness, because what may be known of God is manifest in them, for God has shown it to them. For since the creation of the world His invisible attributes are clearly seen, being understood by the things that are made, even His eternal power and Godhead, so that they are without excuse, because, although they knew God, they did not glorify Him as God, nor were thankful, but became futile in their thoughts, and their foolish hearts were darkened. Professing to be wise, they became fools, and changed the glory of the incorruptible God into an image made like corruptible man-and birds and four-footed animals and creeping things. Therefore God also gave them up to uncleanness, in the lusts of their hearts, to dishonor their bodies among themselves, who exchanged the truth of God for the lie, and worshiped and served the creature rather than the Creator, who is blessed forever. Amen.[220]

Consider this exhortation given by Bill W. of Alcoholics Anonymous to Agnostics and see how it lines up with the exhortation given by Paul in the previous quote from Romans chapter 1:18-23.

---

[220] Rom. 1:18-24.

Hence, we saw that reason isn't everything. Neither is reason, as most of us use it, entirely dependable, though it emanate from our best minds. What about people who proved that man could never fly? Yet we had been seeing another kind of flight, a spiritual liberation from this world, people who rose above their problems. They said God made these things possible, and we only smiled. We had seen spiritual release, but liked to tell ourselves it wasn't true. Actually we were fooling ourselves, for deep down in every man, woman, and child, is the fundamental idea of God. It may be obscured by calamity, by pomp, by worship of other things, but in some form or other it is there. For faith in a Power greater than ourselves, and miraculous demonstrations of that power in human lives, are facts as old as man himself. We finally saw that faith in some kind of God was a part of our make-up, just as much as the feeling we have for a friend. Sometimes we had to search fearlessly, but He was there. He was as much a fact as we were. We found the Great Reality deep down within us. In the last analysis it is only there that He may be found. It was so with us.[221]

God's revelation is not a myth but a reality. No one will be able to say on judgment day that they didn't know about God. God gives many chances to humanity to come into a intimate or personal relationship with Him through His Son. While there is a book in the Bible entitled Revelation, the entire Bible is really the Revelation of Jesus Christ. God created humanity, humanity failed in the Garden of Eden. God had a plan of redemption already in place or He could not be God, because God is Omniscient, Omnipotent, and Omni-present. This merely means that God has all knowledge, all power, and He is everywhere at the same time. Therefore, He had to know that Adam would fail in the Garden, and since God is in complete and total control of everything and everyone, He also has a plan for all that could go wrong in each life of every person ever born. God can cure any ill; He can deliver from any circumstance or situation; He can heal any sickness; He can solve any problem; He can fulfill any need. All of these circumstances and situations are considered the monkey on one's back. God uses Believers

---

[221] Alcoholics Anonymous, We Agnostics 2001, 54-55.

to reveal Himself to Unbelievers by demonstrating His power in their lives when He brings the Believer out of tumultuous storms. If any Believer is in a tumultuous storm and need God to bring him/her out, all one must do is just believe in Him and His power, then watch God go to work. Revelation is displayed and demonstrated that one might believe and be delivered by the awesome power of the living God. Believing in God and His mighty power is what one does to get the monkey off their back. Remember Bill W. of Alcoholics Anonymous and how he was a chronic alcoholic that appeared to be destined to die from alcoholism. Listen to this statement made by the man who pioneered the most successful recovery plan in history:

> The real significance of my experience in the Cathedral burst upon me. For a brief moment, I had needed and wanted God. There had been a humble willingness to have Him with—me and He came. But soon the sense of His presence had been blotted out by worldly clamors, mostly those within myself. And so it had been ever since. How blind I had been. At the hospital I was separated from alcohol for the last time. Treatment seemed wise, for I showed signs of delirium tremens. There I humbly offered myself to God, as I then understood Him, to do with me as He would. I placed myself unreservedly under His care and direction. I admitted for the first time that of myself I was nothing; that without Him I was lost. I ruthlessly faced my sins and became willing to have my new-found Friend take them away, root and branch, I have not had a drink since.[222]

Bill W. understood the reality of being accountable to God, and understood that accountability was exactly what he needed to practice in his life and in all his affairs to be successful in recovery. He humbly offered himself to God to do with him what He would and placed himself unreservedly under God's direction. There is a way to get the monkey off your back, and Bill W. just told you how to get it done. Remember it cannot be done without God; and one has to surrender all that he/she thinks they know and think they can do, and humbly offer themselves to God unreservedly placing themselves in His care

---

[222] Ibid. Bill's Story 2001, 12-13.

and under His direction. Bill W. makes this revelatory statement near the end of the section in the Big Book of Alcoholics Anonymous, "In this book you read again and again that faith did for us what we could not do for ourselves. We hope you are convinced now that God can remove whatever self-will has blocked you off from Him."[223]

Believer's Responsibility

Finally, the responsibility that proceeds conversion and how the Believer exercises their 'Role and Responsibility' before their fellow man and God. The whole idea in this aspect of the experience after conversion is that there is something that Believers do on a daily basis that keeps them connected and walking in the way of the Lord. Bill W. calls it giving back. The biblical exhortation can be found in various verses of scripture, but this one seems to be most appropriate:

"Go therefore and make disciples of all the nations, baptizing them in the name of the Father and of the Son and of the Holy Spirit, teaching them to observe all things that I have commanded you; and lo, I am with you always, even to the end of the age. Amen."[224]

The previous passage suggests that Believers are to get busy reaching out to those who are lost and don't have a relationship with God, and at the same time the promise made by the Lord is that He will be with the Believer to the end of the age or the world as we know it. Since the word of God promises eternal security and a place in His kingdom forever, it's safe to draw the conclusion that He will be with the Believer forever. In the previous passage it is clear that the Lord is referring to the time that the Believer spends on this earth and the task of witnessing to the Unbeliever. Nevertheless, the exhortation and promise is proof that the Believer has a responsibility to minister to humanity. By doing this the Believer stays connected and fulfills the plan and purpose of God to reach out to everyone even if everyone does not receive the message. Bill W. on the other hand takes another approach in his encouragement to those involved in the process of recovery.

---

[223]   Ibid. How It Works 2001, 70-71.
[224]   Matt. 28:19-20.

My friend had emphasized the absolute necessity of demonstrating these principles in all my affairs. Particularly was it imperative to work with others as he had worked with me. Faith without works was dead, he said. And how appallingly true for the alcoholic! For if an alcoholic failed to perfect and enlarge his spiritual life through work and self-sacrifice for others, he could not survive the certain trials and low spots ahead. If he did not work, he would surely drink again, and if he drank, he would surely die. Then faith would be dead indeed. With us it is just like that.[225]

In essence Bill W. is making a statement that Alcoholics in recovery can only keep what they have by giving it away. How much of God is involved in what Bill W. believes about recovery and the process by which he says the alcoholic must live? This is a good question and some reader of this literary work is asking this very question. Well listen to what Bill W. says about the influence that God has in the process of recovery as he knows it.

I was to test my thinking by the new God-consciousness within. Common sense would thus become uncommon sense. I was to sit quietly when in doubt, asking only for direction and strength to meet my problems as He would have me. Never was I to pray for myself, except as my requests bore on my usefulness to others. Then only might I expect to receive. But that would be in great measure. My friend promised when these things were done I would enter upon a new relationship with my Creator; that I would have the elements of a way of living which answered all my problems. Belief in the power of God, plus enough willingness, honesty and humility to establish and maintain the new order of things, were the essential requirements. Simple, but not easy; a price had to be paid. It meant destruction of self-centeredness. I must turn in all things to the Father of Light who presides over us all. These were revolutionary and drastic proposals, but the moment I fully accepted them, the effect was electric. There was a sense

---

[225]   Alcoholics Anonymous, Bill's Story 2001, 14-15.

> of victory, followed by such a peace and serenity as I had never known. There was utter confidence. I felt lifted up, as though the great clean wind of a mountain top blew through and through. God comes to most men gradually, but His impact on me was sudden and profound.[226]

Certainly the previous quote is an extensive one, but much too valuable to be shortened. The value of this information is to set strait the ideology that the Big Book of Alcoholics Anonymous, Bill W. and his cohorts advocated that people choose anything to be their God. With the continual Messianic over-tones and the message of a Savior that Bill W. uses would strongly imply that he was one who believed in not only the Son of God, but God the Son. Recall the verbiage used in the previous quotes, such as:

> My friend promised when these things were done I would enter upon a new relationship with my Creator; that I would have the elements of a way of living which answered all my problems. Belief in the power of God, plus enough willingness, honesty and humility to establish and maintain the new order of things, were the essential requirements.[227]

The word Creator in this previous quote is capitalized to emphasize Messianic implications. The word Creator in the Greek, which is the original language of the New Testament of the Holy Bible is the word **Ktizo**. The phonetics of the word to aid in pronunciation is Ktid'-zo; and give the idea of the proprietorship of the manufacturer; to fabricate, i.e. found (form originally):—create, Creator, make.[228] This information give a more vivid picture of what Bill W. had in mind when he used the verbiage in his statement above. He could not have been talking about just anything or any person that some desperate individual(s) chose to be their god. Listen to the argument of Saint John:

---

[226] Ibid. Bill's Story 2001, 13-14.
[227] Ibid. Bill's Story 2001, 13-14.
[228] Strong's Greek Dictionary s.v. "Creator/Ktizo" (44).

In the beginning was the Word, and the Word was with God, and the Word was God. He was in the beginning with God. All things were made through Him, and without Him nothing was made that was made. "And the Word became flesh and dwelt among us, and we beheld His glory, the glory as of the only begotten of the Father, full of grace and truth.[229]

The God of the Bible is the only one that is referred to by divine design. Not even Darwin was mentioned in the same vernacular when arguing the validity of his theory on creation. The Big Bang Theory is [based] upon a 1955 theory in astronomy: the universe originated billions of years ago from the explosion of a single mass of material so that the pieces are still flying apart—compare STEADY STATE THEORY.[230] Therefore, is it possible that Bill W. could have been referring to anyone other than the God of the Bible? In addition to the responsibility that Believers have for reaching the lost, a continual assessment of their words and action must be called into accountability as well. If one desires to get the monkey off their back, it is a life-long process to live a liberated lifestyle. The Bible presents it to the reader in this manner:

"If we confess our sins He is faithful and just to forgive us our sins and to cleanse us from all unrighteousness. If we say that we have not sinned, we make Him a liar, and His word is not in us."[231] The Big Book of Alcoholics Anonymous presents it to the reader in this manner:

No matter how far down the scale we have gone, we will see how our experience can benefit others. That feeling of uselessness and self-pity will disappear. We will lose interest in selfish things and gain interest in our fellows. Self-seeking will slip away. Our whole attitude and outlook upon life will change. Fear of people and of economic insecurity will leave us. We will intuitively know how to handle situations which used to baffle us. We will suddenly realize that God is doing for

---

[229] John 1:1-3, 14.
[230] Webster s.v. "Big Bang Theory" (149).
[231] 1 John 1:9-10.

us what we could not do for ourselves. Are these extravagant promises? We think not. They are being fulfilled among us—sometimes quickly, sometimes slowly. They will always materialize if we work for them. This thought brings us to *Step Ten*, which suggests we continue to take personal inventory and continue to set right any new mistakes as we go along. We vigorously commenced this way of living as we cleaned up the past. We have entered the world of the Spirit. Our next function is to grow in understanding and effectiveness. This is not an overnight matter. It should continue for our lifetime. Continue to watch for selfishness, dishonesty, resentment, and fear. When these crop up, we ask God at once to remove them. We discuss them with someone immediately and make amends quickly if we have harmed anyone. Then we resolutely turn our thoughts to someone we can help. Love and tolerance of others is our code.[232]

Of course this previous quote is a lengthy one, but necessary to demonstrate the association of recovery with that of salvation and repentance, which should occur on an ongoing basis. Furthermore, prior to reaching the point of *Step Ten* in the Big Book of Alcoholics Anonymous, one should have already completed the first nine steps. This is similar to the process of salvation and progressive sanctification that is associated with the Christian experience of a Believer in Christ. Once an individual experiences salvation, then that person begin participating in activities that fosters growth. Attending Bible study groups, reaching out to others in need, whether that means reaching out to those that are already involved with the church or those who are un-churched. Continuing to take personal inventory by acknowledging sin in one's life and repenting or turning away from that sin. As this process continues over a period of time the individual begin to grow and the struggles become less when coming face to face with temptation and opposition. Once again listen to the exhortation of the Big Book of Alcoholics Anonymous:

---

[232] Alcoholics Anonymous, INTO ACTION 2001, 84-85.

And we have ceased fighting anything or anyone—even alcohol. For by this time sanity will have returned. We will seldom be interested in liquor. If tempted, we recoil from it as from a hot flame. We react sanely and normally, and we will find that this has happened automatically. We will see that our new attitude toward liquor has been given us without any thought or effort on our part. It just comes! That is the miracle of it. We are not fighting it, neither are we avoiding temptation. We feel as though we had been placed in a position of neutrality—safe and protected. We have not even sworn off. Instead, the problem has been removed. It does not exist for us. We are neither cocky nor are we afraid. That is our experience. That is how we react so long as we keep in fit spiritual condition.[233]

Isn't this a wonderful state of mind and condition to be in? What if one could deal with his/her problems with this same mind set. Remember something very crucial to surviving any type of addiction, malady, situation or circumstance; the principles embodied in the plan for recovery outlined in the Big Book of Alcoholics Anonymous really came from the Bible. The principles will work for anyone with any problem. Now the question to the readers of this literary work is, do you want to get the monkey off your back? Just following the simple principles outlined in this book and utilizing the Bible and the Big Book of Alcoholics Anonymous you can achieve recovery from any form of addiction, malady, situation, or circumstance. If you are sick and upon your death-bed and you ask God to heal you, even if you die God has healed you. Listen to what the author of the Revelation has to say about the Eschatological aspects of the new heaven and the new earth:

> Now I saw a new heaven and a new earth, for the first heaven and the first earth had passed away. Also there was no more sea. Then I, John, saw the holy city, New Jerusalem, coming down out of heaven from God, prepared as a bride adorned for her husband. And I heard a loud voice from heaven saying, "Behold, the tabernacle of God is with men, and He will dwell

---

[233] Alcoholics Anonymous 1976, 84-85.

> with them, and they shall be His people. God Himself will be with them and be their God. And God will wipe away every tear from their eyes, there shall be no more death, nor sorrow, nor crying. There shall be no more pain, for the former things have passed away."[234]

Even death will have become something that one can accept, because the eternal security of God will go into effect when death occurs. The death-bed experience and the request for God to heal or deliver will be well understood by the Believer with genuine faith. Therefore, there will be no more fears about sickness, death, or any other circumstance beyond human power, because dependence upon human power is something that the Believer with genuine faith has overcome. Do you really want to get the monkey off your back? If one commits to God's word, God's will, God's work and God's way, then getting the monkey off your back is not only a possibility but a reality. It's going to take total dependence upon God; and not some kind of imaginary god, but the God of the Holy Bible. The God of Abraham, Isaac, and Jacob!

"Now to Him who is able to do exceedingly abundantly above all that we ask or think, according to the power that works in us, to Him be glory in the church by Christ Jesus to all generations, forever and ever. Amen."[235]

---

[234] Rev. 21:1-5.

[235] Eph. 3:20-21.

CHAPTER 8

Family Membership

Family Composition

What a significant element of human existence when considering the composition of the anthropological aspects of various groups of people referred to as the family. According to Webster, one of the definitions of the unit referred to as the family is "a group of people united by certain convictions."[236] Those who believe in a divine designer and also believe that God created everything out of nothing *(Creatio Ex-Nihilo)*, probably believe that humanity is one big family. This reasoning looms out of the biblical account that Adam and Eve were the parents of the entire human race, so in essence humanity is one big family. There are other groups referred to as families, and various church groups refer to themselves as families. Those who are pushing and promoting the Gay and Lesbian agenda refer to two men or two women and a child or children as a family. There are secular 12 Step recovery groups that also refer to themselves as families. Some members of ethnic groups also refer to themselves as a part of a specific family, ethnically. The fact that Webster's definition early on in this chapter stating that the family "is a group of people united by certain convictions," supports the rationale of various groups to define themselves as a family broadens the theory homogeneously of who or what may be considered a family. There are two institutions

---

[236] Ibid. s.v. "family" (448).

in the Bible: First, the family as outlined in the Old Testament in Deuteronomy 6:1-9; and Second, the Church in the New Testament, which is also a family characterized as the Bride of Christ in Ephesians 5:22-33.

Functionality

No family is perfect or totally functional. In every family including the family of God or the body of Christ there are dysfunctional aspects. While some families are biological and others are associated by marriage and relative association, the family is one of the most significant aspects of one's social existence. One can choose what church he/she will attend or where they may place their membership. Alcoholics and Addicts can choose whether to attend and become members of Alcoholics Anonymous, Narcotics Anonymous, Cocaine Anonymous, Gamblers Anonymous, Over-eaters Anonymous, or some other groups not mentioned here, but there are no options for the family one is born into biologically. In any case a family that is functional must have order. In the 12 step recovery groups they classify their organization as a family. There are Secretaries, Chair-persons, Treasurers, General Service Representatives,[237] and so on. Each one has a particular function and is responsible for certain activities. In the biological family there is the Father, Mother, and the Children and each of them have a function to carry out. In the ecumenical family (church) there is the Pastor, Preachers (Associate Ministers), Trustees, Deacons, Deaconess, Ushers, Choir members, and Parishioners[238] and each of these have a particular function. Even the God-head listed in order as is: God the Father, God the Son, and God the Holy Spirit[239] has a particular function that each person of the trinity performs. The God-head is never dysfunctional but is a model or microcosm of what the earthly family should be. When a member of the family is dysfunctional, then problems arise. When one member is self-centered, selfish, or self-seeking, the whole family suffers. Listen to this exhortation from the Apostle Paul on how the family ought to function:

---

[237] Alcoholics Anonymous, Twelve Traditions 2001, 565.

[238] Hiscox 1979, et. al.

[239] Matt. 28:19.

Children, obey your parents in the Lord, for this is right. Honor your father and mother, "which is the first commandment with promise: that it may be well with you and you may live long on the earth." And you, fathers, do not provoke your children to wrath, but bring them up in the training and admonition of the Lord.[240]

Personal Responsibility within the Family

There can be no confusion about the responsibility that each member of the family must carry out to make the family functional. When each member of the family is unwilling to exercise responsibility and do their part to contribute to the over-all duties of the family unit, then there will be discord, strife, and discontentment, ultimately leading to a dysfunctional unit. The reasonable question then would be, how does a family that has fallen into such a pattern of dysfunction survive? The answer will be provided in the next section of this chapter. Concerning the biological family, the responsibility of the father is to attend to the needs of the entire family. The mother and children ought to be able to look to the father of the family unit for provisions and protection. Also, the father should exhibit a godly lifestyle as he models godly conduct and godly principles before the mother and children of his family. The father and mother together will amalgamate forces and train the children by nurturing and admonishing them throughout their maturation process.

Both parents demonstrate how to respond when circumstances and situations ensue that challenge the moral fiber of their individual constitution. The mother will demonstrate to the children what it means to respect those in authority over them by showing respect to her husband as the leader of the family, and the one God holds responsible for how the family lives and carries out its personal business in living a godly lifestyle. The children are to understand their role as subordinates and understand that they have a responsibility to function in such a way that respect for both father and mother is demonstrated by the conduct and behavior toward their parents. Also, children must learn

---

[240] Eph. 6:1-3.

to respect their peers, and this comes as they learn to respect parents, siblings, and extended family members.

Children are suppose to model in the midst of the world what their parents teach them at home, and should be representatives of the conduct and behavior exhibited within the family unit when they are among those outside of the biological family unit. Remember that only God is able to do for those who believe in Him what they are unable to do for themselves, as stated earlier in this literary work by Bill W. of Alcoholics Anonymous.

Much of what is seen among the family today when it comes to addictive behavior is learned behavior, and this means children mimicking the behavior of their parents. If the parents are living a godly lifestyle then mimicking their behavior would be the ideal action desired by the parents as well as society. If the behavior of parents in a family unit is irresponsible and causes a development of anti-social behavior within the children, then seemingly there is the reality of failure; and that failure could mean the self destruction of an individual's life, and have a negative effect on society. Therefore, the family should be a support system that helps the individual members of the family unit to stay connected to the healthy practices and principles in life, found in the word of God. Disrespect of one parent toward the other threatens these principles and lead children astray. When one parent disrespects the other parent, then children are given the perception that respect is not mandatory, but optional. The healthy family that is functional stems from mutual respect of the parents responsible for that family unit. If a family wants to be healthy and functional then the parents must work together and develop a healthy, functional environment that is built upon the foundation of respect. For the one reading this book in a state of desperation and family problems, the process of total surrender and commitment to God will definitely result in getting the monkey off your back.

Membership in the Ecumenical Family

Notice that in spite of the opposition the majority of 12 Step recovery groups have against involvement with religion and faith-based organizations, Bill W. offers this exhortation to those who are part of the A.A. family in becoming a part of another family.

Drinking isolates most homes from the outside world. Father may have laid aside for years all normal activities—clubs, civic duties, sports. When he renews interest in such things, a feeling of jealousy may arise. The family may feel they hold a mortgage on dad, so big that no equity should be left for outsiders. Instead of developing new channels of activity for themselves, mother and children demand that he stay home and make up the deficiency. At the very beginning, the couple ought to frankly face the fact that each will have to yield here and there if the family is going to play an effective part in the new life. Father will necessarily spend much time with other alcoholics, but this activity should be balanced. New acquaintances who know nothing of alcoholism might be made and thoughtful consideration given their needs. The problems of the community might engage attention. Though the family has no religious connections, they may wish to make contact with or take membership in a religious body. Alcoholics who have derided religious people will be helped by such contacts. Being possessed of a spiritual experience, the alcoholic will find he has much in common with these people, though he may differ with them on many matters. If he does not argue about religion, he will make new friends and is sure to find new avenues of usefulness and pleasure. He and his family can be a bright spot in such congregations. He may bring new hope and new courage to many a priest, minister, or rabbi, who gives his all to minister to our troubled world. We intend the foregoing as a helpful suggestion only. So far as we are concerned, there is nothing obligatory about it. As non-denominational people, we cannot make up others' minds for them. Each individual should consult his own conscience.[241]

The Godly Family Unit

What a tremendous exhortation and encouragement from Bill W. and the A.A. Big Book. It should be noted that much of the challenges occurring in family units has to do with the lack of discipline on either

---

[241] Alcoholics Anonymous, The Family Afterward 2001, 131-132.

the parents part when it comes to their own personal struggles, or when it comes to the discipline that parents are to impose upon their children. The ideology of 'Do as I say, not as I do,' does not work with the current generation; moreover, this type of thinking never worked before. This type of thinking would in all appearances contradict the exhortation of the Apostle Paul who offers these words of encouragement: "Imitate me, just as I also imitate Christ."[242] "Therefore be imitators of God as dear children."[243] "Brethren join in following my example, and note those who so walk, as you have us for a pattern."[244] In all the previous quotations from the Apostle Paul's letters is found a common thread of encouragement. That those who are walking with Christ have men and women of God that models the lifestyle they are telling others they need to be living. Another implication here is that it appears to be impossible for parents to be good examples of moral living apart from God. Notice that every form of observation and execution in living properly was connected to a person in relationship with Jesus Christ. How then does any person live a moral lifestyle, or is it possible? Since the Bible tells the reader that "all have sinned and fall short of the glory of God," it is apparent that no one can truly live a moral lifestyle without Jesus Christ as their example, because all have been corrupted by the disease of sin.

Parents' Responsibility to Live Godly

Parents then need to be godly examples unto their children and model the lifestyle and principles that would demonstrate moral, ethical, and godly conduct. What if parents lived such moral lifestyles and they have children that will not follow their example? The writer of the Wisdom Literature of the Bible has the answer for this question as well.

"Train up a child in the way he should go, And when he is old he will not depart from it."[245] According to John MacArthur, there is a process for rearing children with moral, ethical, and godly conduct in mind:

---

[242] 1 Cor. 11:1.

[243] Eph. 5:1.

[244] Phil. 3:17.

[245] Prov. 22:6.

There is only one right way, God's way, the way of life. That way is specified in great detail in Proverbs. Since it is axiomatic that early training secure lifelong habits, parents must insist upon this way, teaching God's Word and enforcing it with loving discipline.[246]

It is hardly possible for parents to teach children God's Word, God's Will, and God's Way if they are not following these principles themselves. So that old adage of 'Do as I say, not as I do,' is obsolete and of no effect when it comes to training someone in the way of life. If a man or woman has children it would benefit them to do just what the writer of the wisdom literature suggested. Should that child or those children turn away from the upbringing that their parents taught and modeled before them, they will at least have the frame of reference in their experience and know how to find their way back. Therefore, the family has challenges all along the way during the years of developmental growth of child rearing and raising of children, but it is the sole responsibility of the parents to do their job in modeling, nurturing, admonishing and disciplining their children. Again, listen to the exhortation of the Apostle Paul concerning children and parent relations:

Children obey your parents in the Lord, for this is right. *"Honor your father and mother,"* which is the first commandment with promise, *"that it may be well with you and you may live long on the earth."* And you, fathers, do not provoke your children to wrath, but bring them up in the training and admonition of the Lord.[247]

There is no doubt in this previous passage that the Apostle Paul was making a statement about the responsibility of both the children and parents. Is it then obvious that it must all begin with the parents and be passed down to the children? This is also true of any group that presents itself as a means of restoration and recovery. Those coming into the group are really seeking direction for their natural lives, whether it

---

[246] MacArthur 1997, notes (22:6—way he should go,)908
[247] Eph. 6;1-4

is a local church body or a 12 Step recovery program. They are looking to those whom were there before they arrived, hoping that a solution to their problem(s) can be revealed by those who have seemingly survived such a demoralizing dilemma. Regardless of whether the challenge is Alcohol, Drugs, Pornography, Gambling, Over-eating, Homosexuality, or some type of emotional disorder, help is available and recovery is possible. All of the various groups mentioned in the previous sentence are also referred to as families. When anyone attends one of the groups mentioned, they find that someone will address the group by referring to those in attendance as family. The church is referred to as a family, and the point here is that regardless of what group is being referred to, the success of the constituents of that group is based upon a relationship with a power greater than themselves. Be realistic, there is only one true power greater than anyone else and that power is God. God cannot be just anything one wants Him to be; and just because someone drops the name God does not mean that they really know or have a genuine relationship with the God of this universe, that created everything and everyone. The reason why people cannot overcome the struggles of life could very well be due to the foundation of their belief system. There are people believing in some type of imaginary power that really has no power at all. Even Satan is able to present himself as an angel of light, when in fact he is darkness.

"And no wonder! For Satan himself transforms himself into an angel of light."[248] "For we do not wrestle against flesh and blood, but against principalities, against powers, against the rulers of the darkness of this age, against spiritual hosts of wickedness in the heavenly places . . ."[249] Now it is true that Satan has more power than people, but he does not have more power than God. Therefore, some people are actually receiving what is passed off as a blessing but it's really a curse from Satan himself. So he enables them to remain abstinent from alcohol, drugs, or some other addictive substance or behavior while all of the time they are living morally deficient lives. They are sleeping with anyone they can get into a bed, they are still lying, cheating, manipulating, and stealing. They are not considering their fellows as Bill W. suggested.

---

[248] 2 Cor. 11:14.
[249] Eph. 6:12.

What kind of family member is it who does not take into consideration his/her brother and sister?

> Now we need more action, without which we find that "Faith without works is dead." Let's look at Steps Eight and Nine. We have a list of all persons we have harmed and to whom we are willing to make amends. We made it when we took inventory. We subjected ourselves to a drastic self-appraisal. Now we go out to our fellows and repair the damage done in the past. We attempt to sweep away the debris which has accumulated out of our effort to live on self-will and run the show ourselves. If we haven't the will to do this, we ask until it comes. Remember it was agreed at the beginning we would go to any lengths for victory over alcohol. Probably there are still some misgivings. As we look over the list of business acquaintances and friends we have hurt, we may feel diffident about going to some of them on a spiritual basis. Let us be reassured. To some people we need not, and probably should not emphasize spiritual feature on our first approach. We might prejudice them. At the moment we are trying to put our lives in order. But this is not an end in itself. Our real purpose is to fit ourselves to be of maximum service to God and the people about us.[250]

Mutual Respect and Consideration for Family

How can anyone who undergoes such rigorous self-searching and self-appraisal continue in the behavior that led to their failure in life? By this time one should have developed a healthy way of living that includes the proper treatment of others as well as self preservation, self respect and dignity. It has been established that people who do not undergo the approach and process of a personal house-cleaning generally go back to what-ever caused there failure in life. When people have not learned how to treat other people, generally they don't know how to treat themselves.

---

[250] Alcoholics Anonymous 2001, 76-77.

> Therefore if there is any consolation in Christ, if any comfort
> of love, if any fellowship of the Spirit, if any affection and
> mercy, fulfill my joy by being like-minded, having the same
> love, being of one accord, of one mind. Let nothing be done
> through selfish ambition or conceit, but in lowliness of mind
> let each esteem others better than himself. Let each of you look
> out not only for his own interests, but also for the interests of
> others.[251]

There is no confusion about the previous passage from the writings
of Paul the Apostle. It clearly indicates that people who know how to
treat others are subject to be in the good graces of God. When Paul
talks about consolation, he is really making a statement that there are
benefits in understanding and carrying out proper treatment of other
people. Consolation merely means that you have comfort. According
to Webster, consolation is "the act for an instance of consoling: the
state of being consoled: COMFORT . . ."[252]

When considering the reality of these findings, it is clear that in
order for the family to be functional they must learn how to treat one
another. Everyone needs family, because family is where an individual's
identity is established. When a person has the saving knowledge of
the Lord Jesus Christ and understanding by adoption[253] that one is
legally apart of God's family, then his/her identity changes. Everyone
wants to belong to someone or something, and when this does not exist
people's lives become meaningless. It is even more significant when
individuals belong to a family with tremendous social, economic, and
intellectual value; and that is exactly what the family of God offers.
God is omnipotent, which means that He is all powerful. "Let the
groaning of the prisoner come before You; According to the greatness
of Your power Preserve those who are appointed to die . . . ."[254]

"And I heard, as it were, the voice of a great multitude, as the sound
of many waters and as the sound of mighty thundering, saying, "Alleluia!

---

[251]   Phil. 2:1-4.

[252]   Webster s.v. "consolation" (280).

[253]   Eph. 1:5.

[254]   Ps. 79:11.

For the Lord God Omnipotent reigns" . . . [255] God is omniscient, which means that He knows everything. "Jesus therefore, knowing all things that would come upon Him, went forward and said to them, "Whom are you seeking?"[256]

After Judas Iscariot had betrayed Jesus and Jesus was approached by those who would take Him into custody, He made the statement above. Now listen to what John MacArthur says about this passage of Scripture.

"Knowing all things. John, in a matter-of-fact way, states that Jesus was omniscient, thus God."[257]

God is omnipresent and everywhere at the same time. When the tragedy of 911 occurred on September 11, 2001, many people questioned God's presence. Where was God; and if He is real how could He allow something like this to happen?

"For the ways of man are before the eyes of the Lord, And He ponders all his paths."[258]

"The eyes of the Lord are in every place, Keeping watch on the evil and the good."[259] God sees everything and everybody as pointed out in the previous quotes, but some people question God's ability to keep control of world events and tragedies. God's will be done is what Jesus said when faced with the reality of death on the Cross.

> Then Jesus came with them to a place called Gethsemane, and said to the disciples, "Sit here while I go and pray over there." And He took with Him Peter and the two sons of Zebedee, and He began to be sorrowful and deeply distressed. Then He said to them, My soul is exceedingly sorrowful, even to death. Stay here and watch with Me." He went a little farther and fell on His face, and prayed, saying, "O My Father if it is possible, let

---

[255] Rev. 19:6.

[256] John 18:4.

[257] John MacArthur, MacArthur Study Bible, (Nashville-London-Vancouver-Melbourne: WORD BIBLES, 1997), John 18:4 study notes.

[258] Prov. 5:21.

[259] Prov. 15:3.

this cup pass from Me; nevertheless, not as I will, but as You will."[260]

God's Sovereign Will

So is God in control of everything or can situations and circumstances subvert God's ability of being in complete control over everything and everybody? In response to the question of God's sovereignty, there are three aspects to God's will. There is God's sovereign will, meaning that under His sovereign will things are certain to happen regardless of what anyone else does or doesn't do in response to God's sovereign will.

> Then God said, "Let Us make man in Our image, according to Our likeness; Let them have dominion over the fish of the sea, over the birds of the air, and over the cattle, over all the earth and over every creeping thing that creeps on the earth. So God created man in His own image; in the image of God He created him; male and female he created them.[261]

This former quote and the following quote are pure examples of God's sovereign will. Two things must be pointed out and the first thing is that God created humanity male and female. The word man in the previous quote is the word Adam in the Hebrew; and the phonetics Aw-dawm which means ruddy [red], a human being (an individual or the species, mankind, etc.): . . . [262] signifies that the male and female were created to be just what God created them to be in the beginning, so how can someone now determine that those caught up in the alternative lifestyle of homosexuality was created in that manner. This position is in direct conflict and contradiction of what Genesis 1:26-27 says about God's creation of humanity. Now here is the second of the two things that must be pointed out concerning the passages in the book entitled Genesis in the Holy Bible.

---

[260] Matt. 26:36-39.
[261] Gen. 1:26-27.
[262] Strong's Hebrew Dictionary s.v. "Man/Adam" (8).

> Then the Lord God took the man and put him in the garden of Eden to tend and keep it. And the Lord God commanded the man, saying, "Of every tree of the garden you may freely eat; but of the tree of the knowledge of good and evil you shall not eat, for in the day that you eat of it you shall surely die.[263]

In this previous quote God is addressing the man Adam concerning his role and responsibility as the over-seer of the garden of Eden. When God gave Adam the command not to eat from the tree in the middle of the garden it was not up for debate. It was God's sovereign will that Adam would not eat from that tree, and Adam was warned of the consequences of doing so. Humanity is warned by God through His word that can be found in the Holy Bible about the consequences of sin. Listen to what God tells the watchman concerning the consequences of sin.

"Behold, all souls are Mine; The soul of the father As well as the soul of the son is Mine; The soul who sins shall die."[264] People ignore the word of God as if it is nothing more than a book for good reading, and that there is no need to adhere to the commandments, instructions and requirements written therein. Judgment Day will be a terrible day for many self-willed individuals, and Judgment Day is part of God's sovereign will. Nevertheless what an all sufficient God that rules over everything and everyone, that in the midst of the sobering reality of Judgment Day He has provided a means by which the sinner can be reconciled to Himself. Therefore, the commandment given Adam in the garden of Eden and the prophecy of the watchman Ezekiel does not have to be the final conclusion to the sinners destiny. Listen to what the Apostle Paul says concerning the solution to the lost individual's tragic position outside of Christ. "For the wages of sin is death, but the gift of God is eternal life in Christ Jesus our Lord."[265] Now this is good news for the Unbeliever. Also, this exhortation is offered to demonstrate that God already had a plan in place for mankind when Adam failed in the garden of Eden, and God was not taken by surprise because He is

---

[263] Gen. 2:15-17.

[264] Ezek. 18:4.

[265] Rom. 6:23.

omniscient. "Therefore, if anyone is in Christ, he is a new creation; old things have passed away behold, all things have become new."[266]

The Apostle Paul emphasizes the newness of re-creation, and he is not talking about a makeover; moreover, he is referring to a radical divine transformation performed by Christ Himself. New creation means a new life, and all of the shame and guilt of acts and events that occurred in the life passed is removed. More importantly the penalty for sin is pardoned and the recipient is rewarded with eternal life in God's kingdom. "The Lord is not slack concerning His promise, as some count slackness, but is longsuffering toward us, not willing that any should perish but that all should come to repentance."[267] Exactly what does this mean? To paraphrase, it simply means that God is not a procrastinator when it comes to keeping his promise but patient with humanity. It is not God's will that anyone goes to Hell; and as a matter of fact God does not send anyone to Hell, but they choose to go when they reject Jesus Christ. Listen to what John MacArthur says about this passage.

> **Not slack**. That is, not loitering or late (cf. Gal. 4:4; Titus 1:6; Heb. 6:18 10:23, 37; Rev. 19:11). **Longsuffering toward us**. "Us" is the saved, the people of God He waits for them to be saved, God has an immense capacity for patience before He breaks forth in judgment (cf. v. 15; Joel 2:13; Luke 15:20; Rom. 9:22; 1 Pet 3:15). God endures endless blasphemies against His name, along with rebellion, murders, and the ongoing breaking of His law, waiting patiently while He is calling and redeeming His own. It is not impotence or slackness that delays final judgment; it is patience. **Not willing that any should perish**. The "any" must refer to those whom the Lord has chosen and will call to complete the redeemed, i.e., the "us." Since the whole passage is about God's destroying the wicked, his patience is not so He can save all of them, but so that He can receive all His own. He can't be waiting for everyone to be saved, since the emphasis is that He will destroy the world and the ungodly. Those who do perish and go to hell, go because

---

[266] 2 Cor. 5:17.

[267] 2 Pet. 3:9.

they are depraved and worthy only of hell and have rejected the only remedy. Jesus Christ, not because they were created for hell and predetermined to go there. The path to damnation is the path of a non-repentant heart; it is the path of one who rejects the person and provision of Jesus Christ and holds on to sin (cf. Is. 55:1; Jer. 13:17; Ezek. 18:32; Matt. 11:28; 13:37; Luke 13:3; John 3:16; 8:21-24; 1 Tim. 2:3,4; rev. 22:17). **All should come to repentance**. "All" (cf. "us," "any") must refer to all who are God's people who will come to Christ to make up the full number of the people of God. The reason for the delay in Christ's coming and the attendant judgments is not because He is slow to keep His promise, or because He wants to judge more of the wicked, or because He is impotent in the face of wickedness. He delays His coming because He is patient and desires the time for His people o repent.[268]

What a wonderful encouragement for those who will comply with the commandments of Jesus' words to Nicodemus,

"Most assuredly, I say to you, unless one is born of water and the Spirit, he cannot enter the kingdom of God. That which is born of the flesh is flesh, and that which is born of the Spirit is spirit. Do not marvel that I said to you, You must be born again."[269] Nothing could explain God's sovereign will better than the previous passages and that is not to say the previous passages are a comprehensive example or reference to the explanation of God's sovereign will, but they do give an example of God's sovereign will.

God's Intentional Will

There is also God's intentional will and this is signified by what God's intentions are concerning what happens. In the Gospel According to St. John and chapter 9, Jesus came upon a man who had been born blind. The disciples asked Jesus why the man was born blind, and if he or his parents had sinned causing the man's blindness. Jesus responded

---

[268] John MacArthur, MacArthur Study Bible, (Nashville-London-Vancouver-Melbourne: WORD BIBLES, 1997), 2 Pet. 3:9 study notes.

[269] John 3:5-7.

to them, "Neither this man nor his parents sinned, but that the works of God should be revealed in him."[270] God allowed the man to be born blind so that Jesus would have opportunity to demonstrate His power when he restored the sight of the blind man. Jesus was aware that everyone in that community knew that the man was born blind, and for those people to witness the miracle of this man gaining sight would be a direct testimony of what God could do; moreover, it had to be God that did it because it took someone beyond human power to carry out such a miraculous work.

> When He had said these things, He spat on the ground and made clay with the saliva; and He anointed the eyes of the blind man with the clay. And he said to him, "Go, wash in the pool of Siloam" (which is translated, Sent). So he went and washed, and came back seeing.[271]

Some people think that the Bible is full of folk tales, and that the miracles never happened. So how do the critics and skeptics successfully refute the resurrection of Jesus Christ? There is no way legitimately that anyone can refute the resurrection of Jesus Christ, because it is clearly specified in God's word that there were absolutely too many witnesses that seen Him alive after He was pronounced dead.

> For I delivered to you first of all that which I also received: that Christ died for our sins according to the Scriptures, and that He was buried, and that He rose again the third day according to the Scriptures, and that He was seen by Cephas, then by the twelve. After that He was seen by over five hundred brethren at once, of whom the greater part remain to the present, but some have fallen asleep. After that He was seen by James, then by all the apostles. Then last of all He was seen by me also, as by one born out of due time.[272]

---

270 John 9:3.
271 John 9:6-7.
272 1 Cor. 15:1-8.

There were those in the blind man's community that refused to believe that this man had been given his sight by the Lord Jesus Christ, and although they knew the man was born blind they just refused to accept the reality that he had been miraculously healed and sight given to one who had never saw anything before. Is the family in disarray, then what is needed is a God that gives sight to the blind. This is what getting the monkey off your back is about.

God's Permissive Will

Then there is God's permissive will, and this is where God permits or allows certain things to happen, so that He has opportunity by way of creating a need to demonstrate His power. Just because God permits or allows evil does not mean that He is the creator of evil. "I form the light and create darkness, I make peace and create calamity; I, the Lord, do all these things."[273] It would appear from the previous quote that God perpetrates evil upon humanity, but nothing could be further from the truth. According to Walvoord and Zuck, God's uniqueness is depicted. There is no one like God and neither can He be competed with, and this is evident in Isaiah "45:5-6, 14, 18, 21-22; 43:11; 44:6; 46:9."[274] "In Cyrus' day the Lord was not universally acknowledged, but eventually He will be (cf. Phil. 2:10-11). People will realize that all that happens—**light** (life), **darkness** (death), **prosperity**, and **disaster** ([**not "evil"**] as in the KJV; cf. Amos 3:6)—comes from God. As the sovereign Lord of the universe He can **do** everything."[275]

Difficulty of God's Permissive Will

Certainly the story has been told many times and most people are familiar with Job's life story recorded in the Old Testament of the Holy Bible in the book entitled Job. Job was a man just and righteous in God's sight. God permitted the devil to have reign upon the earth and as the sons of God presented themselves before the Lord the devil showed up as well. God questioned the devil as to what he was doing

---

273 Isaiah 45:7.
274 Bible Knowledge Commentary O.T. s.v. "Isaiah 45:5-7" (1100).
275 Ibid. "Isaiah 45:5-7" (1100).

and the devil responded going to and fro upon the earth. Then the Lord challenged Satan, saying "Have you considered My servant Job, that there is none like him on the earth, a blameless and upright man, one who fears God and shuns evil?"[276] The devil challenged God to permit or allow him to afflict Job. Then the devil declared unto God that Job would curse Him to His face if he removed Job's hedge of protection provided by God. The Lord allowed the devil to afflict Job by destroying his property and killing all of his livestock. Then the devil caused a storm that killed all of Job's children. After Job would not curse God, then the devil afflicted Job by making him deathly ill. Job's friends turned on him and his wife was telling Job to curse God and die. Job had a very difficult life after the challenge between God and the devil occurred, but Job remained faithful to God after complaining and then realizing that he was in the midst of a test, he surrendered his thoughts and actions totally to God. Job was restored physically, emotionally, and spiritually due to his faithfulness. God gave him twice as many children and livestock as he had before the afflictions of the devil.[277]

Conclusion of the Matter

When the storm rises in the lives of people they need a God that can deliver them. Today when the word of God is read and understood, it refers to those who are a part of God's family and those who are not a part of God's family. It is important to know that one belongs to the first family of the Creator of the universe. It is too great of a gamble to be undecided about such a serious matter when facing eternity and the definitive pending realism of Judgment Day. So there is no mistake about God's will being done; because it certainly will be done. Either it will be done by God's sovereignty, or His intention, or by His permission. It's God's will, and it will be done. It's not God's will that any should perish,[278] and maybe that issue is what makes getting the monkey off your back such a necessity for every reader. How about getting the monkey off your back by obtaining eternal security, and

---

[276] Job 1:8.
[277] Job 1-42.
[278] 2 Pet. 3:9.

knowing your eternal destiny will be with God almighty in heaven? The time is right, and the time is right now! If you have made a decision to make Jesus Christ your Lord, Master, and most of all, your Savior, then turn to Romans 10:9-10, 13. Read and pray a prayer similar to this. Father God, I know that I am a sinner, but I don't want to be anymore. I confess with my mouth that Jesus is Lord over all and believe in my heart that Jesus rose from the dead. Now Lord Jesus please come into my life and forgive my sin, and be my Lord, Master, and Savior. Thank you, Lord Jesus for saving my soul; in Jesus' name I pray. Amen.

If you prayed this prayer, then you have secured eternity with God the Father, God the Son, and God the Holy Spirit. Welcome my brother/sister to the family of God and the body of Christ. May God richly bless everyone tremendously who read and practices the godly principles written in this book.

Benediction

> Now to Him who is able to keep you from stumbling, And to present you faultless Before the presence of His glory with exceeding joy, to God our Savior, Who alone is wise, Be glory and majesty, dominion and power, Both now and forever, Amen[279]

---

[279] Jude 24-25.

BIBLIOGRAPHY

Adams, Jay. Competent to Counsel. Grand Rapids: Baker, 1970, 17-18.

Adam's extraordinarily accurate analysis of the state of counseling in evangelicalism is now more than a quarter of a century old but is more apropos than ever. He has given the Church an indispensable corrective to several trends that are eating away at the Church's spiritual vitality. Christian leaders would do well to heed his still-timely admonition.

Alcoholics Anonymous, *The Story of* How Many Thousands of Men and Women Have Recovered from Alcohol, 3rd. ed. New York City: Alcoholics Anonymous World Services, Inc., 1976.

Alcoholics Anonymous, *The Story of* How Many Thousands of Men and Women Have Recovered from Alcohol, 4th. ed. New York City: Alcoholics Anonymous World Services, Inc., 2001.

Babler, John. *Depression.* Forth Worth, Texas: Southwestern Baptist Theological Seminary, 1999.

Boice, James Montgomery. Foundations of the Christian Faith: A Comprehensive & Readable Theology. Downers Grove, Illinois, USA-Leicester, England: InterVarsity Press, 1986.

Bulkley, Ed. Why Christians Can't Trust Psychology. Eugene, Oregon, HARVEST HOUSE PUBLISHERS, 1993.

Eerdmans, William B. THE EERDMANS BIBLE DICTIONARY. Grand Rapids, Michigan: William B. Eerdmans Publishing Company, 1987.

Enns, Paul. THE MOODY HANDBOOK OF THEOLOGY. CHICAGO: MOODY PRESS, 1989.

Felder, Cain Hope. The Original African Heritage Study Bible: King James Version. Washington, D.C.: The James C. Winston Publishing Company, 1993.

Hiscox, Edward T. The Star Book for MINISTERS. Rev. ed. Valley Forge, PA: JUDSON PRESS, 1979.

MacArthur, John F. The MacArthur Study Bible: New King James Version. Nashville-London-Vancouver-Melbourne: WORD BIBLES, 1997.

MacArthur, John F. Jr., and Wayne A. Mack and others. Introduction to BIBLICAL COUNSELING: A BASIC GUIDE TO THE PRINCIPLES AND PRACTICE OF COUNSELING. Dallas-London—Vancouver-Melbourne: WORD PUBLISHING, 1994.

Martin, Cf. and Deidre Bobgan. PsychoHeresy. Santa Barbara: East Gate, 1987.

McGee, J. Vernon. THRU THE BIBLE: vol. 5, 1 Corinthians through Revelation. Nashville, Tennessee: Thomas Nelson Publishers, Inc., 1983.

Nelson, Thomas. The Holy Bible: New King James Version. Nashville, Tennessee: Holman Bible Publishers, 1988.

Strong, James. STRONG'S EXHAUSTIVE CONCORDANCE: WITH GREEK AND HEBREW DICTIONARY. Nashville, Tennessee: CRUSADE BIBLE PUBLISHERS, INC., 1894.

Greek and Hebrew dictionaries are being utilized as the source for transliterating the original languages of Scripture.

Swindoll, Charles R. GROWING DEEP IN THE CHRISTIAN LIFE: RETURNING TO OUR ROOTS. Portland, Oregon: Multnomah Press, 1986.

Wilson, Bill. 1934 Sober. Wikipedia, 1999-2011. Database on-line. Available from http://reference.findtarget.com.